THE ART OF WILD GAME COOKING

By Eileen Clarke and Sil Strung

Voyageur Press

Edited by Michael Dregni
Designed by Andrea Rud
Printed in Hong Kong

97   98   99   00   5   4   3

Library of Congress Cataloging-in-Publication Data
Clarke, Eileen.
    The art of wild game cooking / by Eileen Clarke and Sil Strung.
            p.   cm. — (The fish and game kitchen)
    Includes index.
    ISBN 0-89658-276-0
    1. Cookery (Game) I. Strung, Sil. II. Title. III. Series.
    TX751.C58 1995
    641.6'91—dc20   95-22060
                                     CIP

Published by
Voyageur Press, Inc.
123 North Second Street, P.O. Box 338, Stillwater, MN 55082 U.S.A.
612-430-2210, fax 612-430-2211

Please write or call, or stop by, for our free catalog of natural history publications. Our toll-free number to place an order or to obtain a free catalog is 800-888-WOLF (800-888-9653).

Educators, fundraisers, premium and gift buyers, publicists, and marketing managers: Looking for creative products and new sales ideas? Voyageur Press books are available at special discounts when purchased in quantities, and special editions can be created to your specifications. For details contact the marketing department.

Page 1: *Venison Kabobs (Photo by Eileen Clarke)*

CONTENTS

Venison Chili Cheese Bake (Photo by Eileen Clarke)

THE ART OF
WILD GAME COOKING

This is a cookbook by hunters who cook what fills their freezers: wild game. And we're not just talking about apartment-sized refrigerator-freezers that hold one deer. Between the two of us, Sil and I own five freezers—and a covey of concrete blocks to keep them shut tight.

It's not just Sil's husband Norm or my husband John who have done the hunting. A friend came to visit our house for the first time recently. John and I were living in a small farming community in central Montana at the time—small, as in 251 people. Rich walked in the door and looked around the living room at the whitetail deer head, the moose antlers, and several European-mount mule deer heads, from spindly 4x4 to nontypical lunker.

"Boy, I wish my wife would let me hang my trophies in the living room," he said.

John smiled. "These *are* my wife's trophies."

I explain this because I've run into so many cookbooks with "game" sections in them where the introduction says something like: "Game was once plentiful in America but now wild herds are much reduced and hunting is a sport enjoyed by the few." And then goes on to suggest that delicate, tender rump steaks should be used for stewing. This was from a recent cookbook, and despite the fact that more deer are killed by motorists than by hunters in Pennsylvania, I can almost forgive the blunder.

I was cooking a turkey the other day, however, looking for a traditional stuffing recipe, and ran across this note about grouse: "Grouse are very dry birds and need larding to make them palatable." The cookbook authors further suggested parboiling each grouse for thirty minutes before broiling. This cookbook was originally published in 1948, when hunting was more than a sport and more than a few people "enjoyed" it. Furthermore, it was published east of the Mississippi where the grouse referred to were not sage or sharptails, which sometimes do need a little help in the kitchen, but the delicate white-meat ruffed and blue grouse.

These kinds of cookbooks make you wonder if the authors have been in the woods, much less ever seen venison or a wild bird on a dinner plate. Many would argue that they love nature, but they're a lot like my brother, Michael, who tells me his neighborhood in Holmes, New York, is similar to Montana. I think about my visit there in 1987, when I suggested taking his kids for a canoe ride on the lake across the street from his house. "Oh no," he said. "You can't do that. We're not members of the Lake Association." I began to understand who usually writes cookbooks.

Sil and I don't run to the custom butcher every time we want to cook duck. We go down to the basement and dig in our freezers. Instead of spring cleaning, we

Montana mule deer (Photo by Eileen Clarke)

do summer cleaning. The last week of August, before upland bird and bow season starts in Montana, we clean out all five freezers, defrost them, and sort the packages as to date and species to make sure nothing goes bad. As I write, we have in our freezers ten species of big game from musk ox to veal whitetail, three of small game, and twelve varieties of birds, including one specklebelly goose from central Alberta (one day's limit).

We eat game. Sometimes our city friends and relatives feel sorry for us and take us out to fancy restaurants for beef. If it's been a while since we last ate beef, which it usually has, the meat tastes rancid to our tongues, and if

Upland bird hunting (Photo by Sil Strung)

we're not wise, we're up all night with indigestion. My husband John likes to tell our hunting friends that I was a vegetarian when he met me. As they smile, waiting for the punch line, I quickly explain: there is no punch line. I was twenty-six, and every time I ate commercial beef I got heartburn, so I quit eating commercial beef. Next time I went to the doctor my blood pressure was down twenty points. A few years later, I started eating nothing but game. I'm twenty-two years older now, eating venison, wild birds, and fish for fifteen of those years, and my blood pressure is still twenty points lower than it was when I stopped eat-

ing beef. Besides, I've never done anything that consumed 100 percent of both mind and body as hunting does.

We eat game. As that dilettante woodsman Henry David Thoreau used to say about firewood, it warms you twice. We stay in shape to hunt, and the meat we bring to the table keeps us healthy. My mother once asked me, "But how do you know where they've been?" Well, *we've* been there. We've sat at the base of a grizzled old cottonwood tree listening to the owls going to bed as the deer awaken from theirs. We've walked the game trails in the mountains chasing after elusive elk. These are much nicer places than any feed lot or dairy farm I've ever seen where the cows are up to their tail roots in mud, manure, and urine. It's a lot quieter than the poultry slaughterhouses where my mother used to buy chicken.

We eat game. A friend came to my house and hunted for a week, each night watching my husband, John, and me cook venison steaks, roasts, Stroganoff, stir-fry. At the end of the week, he said in a surprised tone, "Why you people treat it like real meat!" It is real meat. We are real people cooking it. With tender loving care and five real freezers in the basement.

Welcome to *The Art of Wild Game Cooking*.

BIG GAME

From Shot to Gambrel

The three most important factors after the shot are time, temperature, and cleanliness. If your venison tastes off, then there's a good chance one of these factors is to blame. Generally, cleanliness affects flavor and temperature affects taste, but they often overlap and it's hard to talk about one without talking about the other. And time? Time rules over all.

Skinning

I have a friend who always skins the carcass immediately after field dressing. I've walked into his camp when it was only 15°F (-9°C) and there's his deer, elk, sheep, whatever, hanging from a meat pole in a cheap muslin nightgown. (Good thing it's cold because cheap bags don't keep the bugs out.) A lot of people think that's normal, but all he's done is removed the animal's own sterile game bag and replaced it with a manmade one, one that is not nearly as sturdy and will not keep the carcass from drying out.

Let me tell you what I do. First I clean as much blood out of the body cavity as possible. If there's snow on the ground, I throw several handfuls inside and wipe it along the inside of the rib cage and pelvis; if I'm near a stream, I drag the carcass into it, allowing the current to wash through the length of the animal for several minutes. Prairie hunting, where the streams dry up months before big-game season starts and there's usually not enough snow to build a snowmouse, I carry two five-gallon (19-liter) water jugs in the vehicle. I pour at least two gallons (7½ liters) of water into the cavity, and then lift the animal by the shoulders and drain it out through the split pelvis. Then I do it again. I'm not only cleaning the blood out, but also all the other debris that affects taste, especially the animal's own hair.

The second thing I do is remove the fillets from along the inside of the spine—they run along the top of the ribcage inside the animal—drop them in a plastic bag, and put them on ice. Fillets are the most tender cut of meat on any animal, and they dry out quickly. Then, I rinse off the liver and heart and put them on ice, too. Many books tell you to cut out the musk glands first, then use that same knife to field dress and skin the animal. This procedure only takes the musk that you were trying to get rid of in the first place and introduces it to the entire carcass. It's one of the fastest ways to make the meat taste bad.

Next, I drag the animal home, or to the vehicle, and hang it, still with the skin on. Take the skin off and the flies can get at it. Take the skin off and the meat starts drying out, not just where you had to open the animal to field dress it, but over the entire outer surface. When you butcher, you'll have to cut all that away. I don't know about you, but I work too hard to give perfectly good meat to the magpies.

So when do you skin an animal? When it's warm. Problem is, if it's warm enough to skin the animal, it's probably warm enough that you have to take other measures as well. My friend Buck shot a bull moose three years ago, twelve miles (19 km) back in a no-vehicle area. It was a warm September morning; the sun hadn't made it into the narrow mountain valley yet, but it soon would, and the weatherman had forecast a high of 82°F (28°C). Buck started by field dressing and dragging the entrails clear. Then he skinned the moose, belly up, and laid the skin out around the carcass, being careful not to step on it or drag dirt onto it. He quartered the animal, laid the quarters out on the hide and reduced the quarters further. He removed the shoulder from the rib cage, the lower legs from the shoulder and so on, eventually ending up with twelve transportable pieces, including head, neck, and hide. Then, before he took the first load out and got help, he built a make-shift platform over the creek out of fallen alder. He spaced the meat out on the platform and loosely covered it with leafy boughs. The loose covering provided more shade and protected the meat from birds, while the platform and the spacing of the meat allowed air to circulate and cool down the meat. Just removing the hide would not have been enough.

On the other hand, my husband John shot a bull elk opening day of bow season, September 1. It was a hot day, but he took the bull at last light. That night, and the several nights before, the temperature had gotten down to 50°F (10°C). John hung the bull—with a little help from a friend's front-end loader—in our barn. The night temperature cooled the animal down, even with the skin on, and the shade of the barn kept the animal cooling during the day.

John could have skinned the bull. But in September, before the first hard frost hits, bugs are a problem. He knew the 50°F (10°C) night would be sufficient to cool the bull down properly, and skinning the

Previous page: *Whitetail deer (Photo by Erwin and Peggy Bauer)*

Caribou bull (Photo by John Barsness)

animal would only leave it open to flies. Skinning was just more work, and it would be bad for the meat.

Cooling the Carcass

The vital thing for all game animals—skinned or not—is to cool the carcass within the first twenty-four hours after the shot to an optimum temperature of 32–55°F (0–2°C). Just as important is to get the cooling process started within the first four hours. In the case of John and his bull elk, skinning wasn't necessary. Skinning wasn't enough with Buck and his bull moose. When it's warm enough to skin, skinning is *often* not enough.

Large animals—bull elk, moose, musk ox—are more difficult to cool down than small animals, but there are a couple of things you can do to help them along when it's not quite warm enough to have to skin and quarter. Many people think the hindquarters are the first part to spoil, but on large animals it's actually the front quarters. The reason? First, there's a lot more bulk on the front. Second, if you intend to mount the head, you don't cut into the cape. That leaves the neck, head, and shoulders as a block, which has only one opening

and no free air circulation. So what do you do?

If it's not a trophy head, begin by splitting the rib cage from the sternum (the breast bone). Standing astride the animal's chest, take a sturdy knife in both hands and place it left or right along the side of the sternum. Now, slowly pop the cartilage connection between each rib and the sternum. This is easiest to do on a young animal; like humans, the older the animal, the more this cartilage has ossified into hard bone. If you have trouble with a knife, do it with a small saw. Then remove the esophagus (it's the ringed tube inside the upper chest cavity), neck, and head from the front quarters. You have now opened the front quarters to good air circulation and did not have to quarter and skin.

A trophy animal is a bit trickier. When they skin a trophy head, taxidermists make the cut up the backbone, just up to between the ears. If you want to save the cape, that's where you make the cut. Beginning below the front shoulders, slit the hide up along the spine to where the neck joins the head. Then, carefully skin the hide down from the spine—leave some meat on the hide rather than risk cutting it—and separate the head from the carcass. Let the taxidermist skin everything forward of the ears. Now fold the hide back on itself, inside to inside, so it doesn't dry out. Then remove the esophagus; it will be much easier to grasp now rather than reaching up through an unsplit ribcage.

Now that you have the inside of the carcass completely open, hang the animal to allow air to circulate freely around the outside as well. If you're in camp, hang it from a tree or erect a tripod of tree limbs to hang it. If you're going to be driving home in those first twelve hours, lay the carcass over some wooden boards or other hard, narrow object to keep air circulating under the animal. When I first came to Montana twenty-five years ago, a lot of folks liked to strap their deer across the hood of their car. You don't see that much anymore, which is good because the engine will not let the animal cool properly. And don't lay two animals close enough to touch. Neither one of them will cool.

Cold Shortening

As important as it is to cool an animal down quickly, it's equally important not to let the carcass freeze in those first few hours. About twelve years ago, John took a forkhorn mule deer in the Missouri Breaks on a bitterly cold day. He left the meat hanging outside overnight, as he'd always done. It should have been a tender buck, but after aging it for a week at 55°F (13°C), the most tender steaks were tough as nails. It's called cold shortening. If the carcass freezes in that first twelve hours, the meat toughens up and nothing you do will repair the damage.

So there you are, on top of a mountain in the cold with an animal down. Let's assume you can't get it safely indoors before it freezes solid, or build a fire and hang out with it for twelve hours. What do you do? I had a friend who lost a deer on a cold November night. Knowing he'd made a killing shot, and being a careful person anyway, he got up early the next morning and searched for the animal. It took him four hours, in below-zero weather, searching a thick river bottom. The buck had fallen within seventy-five yards (68 m) of where it was shot, and had been dead for more than twelve hours, but he'd fallen on his stomach, his legs tight against the chest trapping his body heat inside. No cold shortening.

The best thing to do is imitate that deer. Once you've field dressed the animal, take it apart one quarter at a time, as you're ready to take that quarter out of the woods. Leave the rest of the animal whole, on its belly, and cover it with a tarp, or even a space blanket if you're carrying a spare, and tuck it tightly around the carcass to trap the body heat. You only need to keep the carcass from freezing for the first twelve hours; after that cold shortening is not a factor.

Muscle Shortening

There's a twist on cold shortening that has nothing to do with temperature, and if you're fortunate enough to always take the meat out in quarters or better, you'll never run into it. It doesn't even have a name. It just makes the meat tough. Let's call it muscle shortening.

Muscle shortening occurs when you bone the meat out in the first twelve hours. When you not only remove the major muscle groups from the bones, but cut across the grain, it allows the meat to contract, and it never, never relaxes again. Like cold shortening, once the meat is muscle shortened, you can't age it long enough to make it tender. Cut with the grain, and take out the meat in the largest chunks possible.

In short, keep the hide on if it's cold; keep the hide on if it's below 80°F (27°C); keep the hide on if it's above 80°F (27°C) but going to start cooling down in the next couple of hours. But if you know it's going to be hot, and you're not near water, carry good-quality, muslin-type game bags, a saw, and lots and lots of patience.

If your hunting area has clean, cold water, bring along some large plastic bags to cool the meat in hot weather. You can put the quartered meat in sealed bags and put the bags in the stream to cool the meat down. But be cautious in the use of plastic with fresh killed meat. Never put fresh meat in plastic unless you're putting it into very cold water, or you know it will be back out, and cooling down, in one hour or less. Time is a machine that stops for no one, no where.

Hanging the Carcass

Bring your kill home as soon as possible. Like a rancher butchering an Angus steer, you can control more of the environment on your home turf. When we get home from a successful hunting trip, the first thing we do is back the truck up to the barn and hang the animal. Might as well do it while you're in your grubby clothes, and, admit it, the most important cargo you've got is the meat.

In our barn, there's a rope that hangs from a roof

beam, and a gambrel from the rope. A friend made two gambrels for us several years ago: the deer-sized gambrel is a twenty-four-inch-long (60-cm) steel bar with a horseshoe welded to one end, stationary. He attached a second horseshoe to the other end with three links of heavy chain. You slip the welded shoe to one hock and slide the chain shoe into the other hock. Then drive the truck away, and *Voilà!* I'm usually standing too close and get whacked in the shoulder as the animal swings free. But the gambrel holds.

A lot of people prefer to hang their deer head up; we do it head down, nose just above the ground. It really doesn't matter. We find it easier to skin, later, when it's hung by the rear legs.

Second thing we do when we get home? Easy. A hot shower. (Well, after we put the heart and fillets in the refrigerator and the liver to soak in cold water. It always seems like the shower comes second.)

Once you get the meat safely hung in your garage, barn, or cooler, the hard, gritty, man-against-nature battle is over. Now it's intellectual: All you've got to worry about is aging it properly, and deciding what grade of meat you've got. Take one last look around your hunting spot. Is it lush or dusty; grass up to your shoulders or spotty at best? It will all help you decide later how to handle the meat. And besides, that's what you're out there for. If you'd just gone to Safeway, it would have been a lot easier, but not nearly as much fun.

From Gambrel to Table

All game animals, except antelope and the young of the year, grow more tender with careful aging, just as any commercially raised animal. Antelope—young or old, male or female—don't benefit from aging because they have little collagen, the connective tissue in the meat fiber that aging breaks down. Let's put to rest right now that old myth that aging is the rotting of meat. It's not. Aging is the breakdown of collagen; if the meat rots, you've gone way too far. That's the who and why of aging. The what, when, where, and how take longer to explain.

Testing the Meat

Last summer John and I spent several days in the Arctic in an Inuit summer camp. John was hunting musk ox; I was supposed to hunt caribou. We'd meet up later to fish for Arctic char. I ended up with an extremely painful and virulent case of shingles instead, and spent the entire time in the Arctic in camp—on my back. This may sound like a total waste of time, but this was not an ordinary hunting camp.

This Inuit summer camp included kids and grandparents, wives and sisters, and while the elders and their minions guided John and his fellow healthy hunters, I lay back in camp being watched over by everyone else—mostly our cook and all the children. Since I wasn't hunting or fishing, the women thought I was as traditional as they were and accepted me—however conditionally—as one of their own. My status improved enormously one nasty, wet afternoon.

In the Arctic, sounds travel, and when you're laid up, you listen hard. So the afternoon the motor boat showed up with John and his musk ox, I had been waiting on the shore for twenty minutes already. His guide, David, was grinning with pride at the skill of "his hunter" and the size of his trophy. It was an old musk ox. Another hunter had passed him up because one horn was broomed and it wouldn't have placed in his trophy club book. John has a habit of finding those animals, and relishing their distinctive trophies.

As the men carried the musk ox, quarter by quarter, up to a large blue tarp on shore, the thing I noticed was that the animal had no fat reserves. It worried me, given the age and sex of the musk ox, and I leaned over one of the hind quarters and sniffed at the meat. It was fresh and sweet, like young whitetail. I smiled with relief, and noticed as I turned back to John to comment, that the Inuits, wives and children, guides and old men, were smiling with me.

It was good meat. And I was a good person for checking the meat first.

You know what good meat is. You've seen it at the grocery store—or at least the appearance of it. Good meat is red in color, does not feel slimy to the touch, and has no rancid odor. Next time you're at the grocery store compare the meat they call "fresh" with the meat they're discounting for quick sale. The discounted meat is browner, has either a dried or slick appearance and has a rancid odor even when it's still edible. When it's not edible, it's even more noticeable. So look, touch, and smell the animal the first chance you get; then start deciding how you need to care for it.

All game animals follow the same anatomy as beef: the backstraps, tenderloin, and upper rump are the most tender. The back end of the tenderloin is more tender than the front; the rear quarters more tender than the shoulder quarters. From backbone to knee (top to bottom) you cut steaks and roasts; below the knee is tough, sinewy stuff, good for stew meat. As a rule, even if the stew meat is gamy tasting, the pure muscle cuts—roasts and steaks—can be tasty. It's the fat and sinew that hold the bad flavors, not the meat itself (although sometimes you can get real unlucky and the whole animal is saturated with that musty taste).

Once you have examined the exterior, slice off a small piece of shoulder steak—a couple of ounces—and cook it up in the broiler, or pan fry it on medium-high with just a little oil in the pan. The first thing you're looking for is taste; second is tenderness. John shot a Russian boar in California a few years ago. The boar had 2¾-inch-long (7-cm) tusks, so we were prepared for him to be tough. But as our guide skinned the animal and quartered it in the camp's screened-in meat locker, he made a suggestion for taste-testing the meat. "Don't cook it in your favorite pan," Greg told us. "In fact, take the barbecue out back in the alley as far from the house as you can get." An involuntary shiver worked up his muscular back all the way up to the top of his shaved head. "Old boars are bad stuff. Yeah, man, put the barbecue out in the alley, and be prepared to duck and cover."

We took his advice. The neighbors thought we were crazy barbecuing in a snowstorm, but the boar tasted fine. Tough as nails, and never got better, but it tasted fine. Guides have a paranoiac/covetous streak that's sometimes hard to read. I believe Greg honestly believed we'd have bad-tasting boar. But those guys in the Arctic said the same thing about John's musk ox.

"Bad meat," they said in English far better than my Inuit. "Very bad meat. Old bulls taste terrible."

We smiled and nodded politely, then cut out both tenderloins and a rear quarter anyway and wrapped them in the hide. Our plan was to let them cool down overnight, then wrap them in plastic for our return trip and leave the rest of the meat for the camp. That was the plan. In the morning, one tenderloin was gone.

The point is, listen to the guides, but take the meat out anyway. Let the cook sort it out later.

So how was that shoulder steak you tested? Was it sweet and mild? Did you make the whole kitchen smell like road kill? Or was it somewhere between OK and not what you'd hoped? If it wasn't too bad, there are ways to cook steaks and roasts to hide a moderate gamy taste: the recipes for Punk Roast, Cajun Roast, and Tommy's Tacos are only three included in these pages.

But if the top of the shoulder is off, most of what you would use for burger and stew will be worse, and the longer you store the meat in the freezer, the more those flavors develop. After six months to a year in your freezer, the flavor even metamorphoses into a weird, slimy texture in the sinew.

Take another bite of that steak and ask yourself: Am I going to look forward to digging a chunk of this out of the freezer come June? (Remember this is strictly a taste test so far.) If the answer is Yes, good. If the answer is Maybe or No, consider the options. You can take the burger and stew meat to the sausage maker now, or wait six months and see if you start digging under and around those packages. You can still take them to the sausage maker in June. Unless I find an animal that's really gamy, that's what I do. The sausage maker isn't as busy then, and you have more chance your meat won't get mixed up with everyone else's as sometimes happens in the heat of the season. In the meantime, trim the steaks and roasts ruthlessly, removing all fat before freezing them.

Let's assume the taste is good. How easily does the test steak cut? Did you cut it with a fork, or did you have to take out your Swiss Army knife? You shouldn't need a steak knife for wild meat any more than you should need one for domestic. If you couldn't cut it easily, you need to hang it for a while. You need to age it.

Aging Meat

Here's where time becomes a major player again. Time and temperature. Remember the movie *Rocky*, when Sly Stallone was working out in the meat locker, punching the sides of beef as if they were heavy bags? Now take Sly Stallone out of the picture, and that's aging: whole carcasses hanging in a clean, controlled-temperature environment. Optimum temperature is below 55°F (13°C) but above freezing. Freeze the carcass and the whole process stops. Get it too warm, and the meat will sour or rot. Time and temperature. Other than those two, aging is a simple process.

Sil has the most perfect non-commercial aging facility I know. It's a three-car garage, attached to her house. It has a wood stove to keep the temperature above freezing, and the whole structure stands at six-thousand feet (1,800 m) above sea level. The combination of altitude, a large stand of old cottonwoods shading the garage, and the garage's own insulation keeps the temperature inside below 70°F (21°C), even in those first hot days of early bow-hunting season. In the heat of battle, I've seen as many as twelve animals hanging from the rafters: Sil's, Norm's, mine, John's, their other visiting friends, and neighbors up and down the canyon. There's also running water: when I killed my Shiras moose one canyon over from Sil's house, it was there I took it, immediately, to wash off the dirt and hair, then hang it out of the sun. That's the danger of having too deluxe an aging facility. Everyone comes. But you can do with less. Running water, a place to hang the animal so that it's not touching anything else, and shade. If you have a source of heat, so much the better.

What *is* an absolute necessity is that you keep track of the temperature, day and night, and check the animal at least once a day. If it's over 60°F (15°C), check the animal at least twice daily: first thing in the morning, and again midday. When I shot that moose, even Sil's perfect garage was a little warm. Daytime temperatures reached 60°F (15°C) inside, then cooled down to 45°F (7°C) at night. At that temperature, the process gallops. We checked the moose breakfast, lunch, dinner, and bedtime. Granted it was a young bull, but by the morning of the third day, a slight tinge of mold had appeared on the edge of the exposed ribcage. We butchered that day.

In moderate to cold temperatures—a fairly constant 35–40°F (1½–4½°C)—an animal will age safely seven to ten days. (I've left some animals up to twenty-one days. I'd only recommend that after you have some experience judging the meat.) But don't set your seven-day timer and forget it no matter how cool it is. Every animal is different. Every climate is different. You want to leave it as long as you can, especially if that test steak was tough, but do not let the mold get a good start. (Mold actually has nothing to do with aging; you just don't want it to form.) If you're nervous about letting your trophy hang, cut a small steak each morning and test it. But remember: If the meat was cold shortened, muscle shortened, or just an old tough animal, it may never get fork tender. Look at it, smell it, touch it, and always err on the side of caution. Once mold appears anywhere, you must butcher immediately.

In super cold, as it sometimes gets in Montana in November, the problem is keeping the aging process going. A couple of years ago, I shot a young 4x4 mule deer. We brought him home on a balmy October afternoon, but within a couple of days, the temperature dropped below zero and the deer froze solid. Over the course of the next three months, we had a few warm days, but my deer never thawed out: We'd check it every couple of days—go out and knock on it—but it was always hard as a rock. Finally, in March, it thawed and we butchered it right up. Our friends were shocked. That meat's no good, they kept saying, no matter how many times we told them it was tender. But it was. Frozen meat doesn't decay. It might dry out, but since we left the hide on that wasn't a problem. It was nerve-racking though. We couldn't go anywhere without checking the weather carefully to make sure the animal wouldn't thaw while we were gone. Time and temperature.

One more thing about aging. You'll hear people say they never age their meat and it tastes fine. The question is, How long did it take you to get the animal out of the woods, and how long did it sit around at home before you butchered it? Aging starts as soon as *rigor mortis* leaves the carcass—usually within twelve hours. So if you took the afternoon to get home, then slept all night, you aged the animal. Young animals don't take much. If you have a small buck, or the doe's teeth aren't worn or stained, it's young and tender already, and it won't take much more than overnight to age it. It's the older animals—and you can tell by the stained and worn-down teeth and the size of the antlers if your animal is more than a year or two old—who need to hang one to seven days. When you're not sure, do the steak test.

A lot of people read and write philosophically and esoterically about big-game hunting. Here's what I think: Dead is dead. Animals don't read Ortega Y Gasset or care one way or the other who shoots them. But I care. I spent years perfecting a heart-lung shot that didn't waste any meat or make the animal suffer needlessly, only to realize that if I didn't at least clip the shoulder the animal could dive into a thick coulee and never be found. So now I waste that five pounds (2¼ kg) of meat so I can see the animal go down, and I take it out on the other end. I don't skin in cool weather; I don't high-grade—taking only the steaks and roasts. But I trim ruthlessly, both fat and blood-shot meat, so that no animal suffers that final degradation: freezer burn. (Followed, inevitably, by being fed to the dogs.) And over the years, Sil and I have both worked hard to find and perfect recipes not only for the sweet tender meat but remedies for those few animals that still end up gamy.

RECIPES FOR TOUGH AND STRONG-TASTING MEAT

Ungulates are all venison: deer, antelope, musk ox, elk, red stag. More than the species, what is important when matching animal to recipe is the cut, the tenderness, and the taste. If the meat is tender, cook it quick and dry; if it's tough, cook it long and wet. Look for recipes with hearty flavors and spices that will mask a gamy flavor. If it overpowers these recipes, you should probably make it into sausage.

Recipes for Gamy Meat

John's Punk Buck Roast
Cajun Venison Roast
Tommy's Tacos
Sauerbraten
Venison Asado
Cowboy Steaks with Sawmill Gravy
Antelope Stir-fry
Citrus Pot Steaks
Easy Breakfast Sausage
Easy Cajun Sausage
Sil's Slow Cook Spaghetti Sauce
Eileen's Quick Spaghetti Sauce
North Country Chili
Chili Cheese Bake
Montana Creole Pie
Mexican Fiesta Casserole
Traditional Jerky
Burger Jerky
Burgundy Bear

Recipes for Tough Cuts

Citrus Pot Steaks
Potsdam Stag Roll
Venison Swiss Steak
Cowboy Steaks with Sawmill Gravy
Tommy's Tacos
Venison Asado
Sauerbraten
Venison Au Jus
Any burger, soup, or stew recipe

STEAKS

ANTELOPE PEPPER STEAK

Yield: 3–4 servings

This is an ideal quick, dry-fried method for cooking large, tender steaks.

Pressing the peppercorns into the venison for Antelope Pepper Steak (Photo by Sil Strung)

Ingredients
2 tablespoons fresh peppercorns
1–1½ pounds (½–¾ kg) round steak, cut
   1 inch (2½ cm) thick
salt, to taste
½ cup (125 ml) butter
2 tablespoons lemon juice
1 teaspoon Worcestershire sauce
Fresh parsley

Cooking
1. Run the peppercorns through a blender on coarse setting. With the palm of your hand, press the pepper into both sides of the steaks.
2. Heat a heavy iron skillet on high heat setting, sprinkle salt in the bottom, and brown both sides of the meat. Reduce heat to medium and continue cooking until desired doneness, approximately 3–5 minutes a side.
3. When the steaks are almost done, add butter, lemon, and Worcestershire sauce to the pan and bring to a boil. Place the steaks on a serving platter and pour the butter mixture over the top. Garnish with fresh parsley.

Antelope buck (Photo by Erwin and Peggy Bauer)

Venison Kabobs

Yield: 2–3 servings

This is a great way to use choice scraps of meat—pieces that can be cut across the grain but are too small to be considered for a roast or steak. Although kabobs are traditionally cooked on skewers, we've found this method a nuisance. The fresh vegetables split off the shaft, and you can't get the mushrooms and potatoes to stay put no matter what you do. So instead of cooking the meal on a skewer, we put the venison, bacon, and raw vegetables in a hinged grate (actually a 9x13-inch/22x32-cm, six-patty burger grate) and cook the rest separately.

Venison chunks in marinade for Venison Kabobs (Photo by Sil Strung)

Venison Kabobs on the barbecue (Photo by Sil Strung)

Marinade Ingredients

1 cup (250 ml) Burgundy or other dry red wine
½ cup (125 ml) soy sauce
1 tablespoon curry powder
¼ teaspoon ground ginger
1 clove garlic, minced
1 pound (½ kg) venison

Kabob Ingredients

4 tomatoes, sliced
2 green peppers, sliced
2 onions, sliced
1 zucchini, sliced
1 pound (½ kg) bacon
20 whole mushrooms
15 small whole potatoes, parboiled and drained
3 tablespoons butter
Garlic salt, to taste

Preparation

1. Combine wine, soy sauce, curry powder, ginger, and garlic in a medium-sized bowl and mix well. Cut the venison into 1 inch (2½ cm) cubes and add to the marinade. Marinate for 2 hours, stirring occasionally.

Cooking

1. Fire up the barbecue. If you have propane, pre-heat on high for 10 minutes, then turn down to medium. As the barbecue gets hot, place venison, tomatoes, peppers, onions, and zucchini on a hinged grate. Lay the bacon strips over the top.

2. Barbecue the kabobs over white-hot coals. The meat is done when the bacon no longer spits fat and the very edges of the fresh vegetables begin to blacken.

3. While the kabobs are barbecueing, quickly sauté the mushrooms and parboiled potatoes in the butter and garlic salt, and keep warm.

4. To serve, release the contents of the grate onto a serving platter and pour the mushroom-potato mixture over the top.

BLACK AND BLUE VENISON STEAKS

Yield: 4–6 servings

Grilling a steak over coals is by far my favorite method. To achieve the black and blue effect you must get the propane cooker at the hottest temperature possible by preheating the barbecue on high for at least 10 minutes. When using charcoal, have the coals a glowing cherry red.

Always use tongs when turning the meat. A fork pierces the meat, pouring all the seared-in juices onto the coals; tongs will keep the juices where they belong.

Ingredients

1 teaspoon garlic salt
Pinch of ground oregano
Pinch of powdered thyme
Pinch of ground allspice
1 teaspoon pepper
$\frac{1}{4}$ cup (60 ml) melted butter or margarine
2–3 pounds (1–1 $\frac{1}{2}$ kg) boneless venison round steak, 1 inch (2 $\frac{1}{2}$ cm) thick

Cooking

1. Combine the seasonings with melted butter and brush the steaks liberally with this butter mixture. Place the meat on the preheated barbecue.
2. Keep track of the time until the blood starts to seep from the top side of the meat. As soon as blood appears, turn the steak over and cook it for half the time you clocked for the first side.
3. Finish off by basting both sides with the butter, then return the steak to the barbecue for a quick sizzle. This will result in a steak with rare meat in the center and medium rare around the edges.

Black and Blue Venison Steaks (Photo by Sil Strung)

Antelope Stir-Fry with Vegetables

Yield: 3–4 servings

Stir-frying is the Chinese way of cooking meats and vegetables quickly in a small amount of oil over high heat. A wok is the perfect stir-frying tool—although you can use a heavy skillet or Dutch oven. Peanut oil is ideal for stir-frying as it won't smoke at high temperatures.

Antelope Stir-Fry with Vegetables (Photo by Sil Strung)

Marinade Ingredients

1 pound (½ kg) boneless round or shoulder steaks
1 tablespoon peanut oil or vegetable oil
1 teaspoon cornstarch
½ teaspoon sugar
1½ teaspoons soy sauce
Dash of pepper

Stir-fry Ingredients

¼ cup peanut or vegetable oil
1 teaspoon ginger root, finely chopped
3 cloves garlic, minced (about 1 teaspoon)
½ pound (250 g) broccoli, chopped
½ pound (250 g) snow peas
3 stalks celery, chopped
½ teaspoon salt
½ cup (125 ml) chicken broth
2 tablespoons corn starch
¼ cup (60 ml) cold water
2 tablespoons oyster sauce
3 green onions

Preparation

1. Cut away any fat or gristle from the meat. Cut the meat with the grain into 2-inch (5-cm) strips; then across the grain into ¼-inch (½-cm) slices. These cuts are a little easier to make if the meat is still slightly frozen.
2. Mix the marinade ingredients well in a glass bowl and add the meat, making sure to coat the meat evenly on all sides with the marinade mixture. Cover with plastic wrap and refrigerate for at least 20 minutes.
3. Cut all the vegetables into approximately the same size pieces and set aside. Remove the venison from the marinade and drain if necessary.

Cooking

1. Heat the wok to high and add 2 tablespoons oil, rotating the wok to coat all sides. Add the venison, ginger root, and garlic, and stir-fry until the meat turns brown, about 2–3 minutes. Remove from the wok and set aside.
2. Add 2 more tablespoons of peanut oil to the wok; add broccoli, snow peas, celery, and salt, stir-frying over medium-high for 1 minute. Add chicken broth; heat to boiling. Stir in venison; heat once again to boiling. Combine cornstarch with water. Add to the wok and cook until the sauce is thickened, about 15 seconds. Stir in oyster sauce and garnish with green onions. Serve over rice.

VENISON FONDUE

Yield: ⅓–½ pound (165–250 g) of venison per person

This is a fun way of preparing venison. You provide the fondue pot, meat, and sauces, gather some friends, and let them do the cooking. If you don't have a fondue pot you can use an electric frying pan, chafing dish, or wok.

Ingredients
½ pound (250 g) venison per person
2 cups (500 ml) peanut oil

Cooking
1. Trim and cut the venison into 1-inch (2½-cm) cubes.
2. Heat peanut oil in fondue pot to boiling. Remove from the stove and place the pot on the fondue stand in the middle of the table.
3. Each guest places their own meat cube on their fondue fork, dips it into the hot oil to cook it; very rare takes only a few seconds. The meat can then be dipped into a sauce. Two good commercially prepared sauces are horseradish sauce and A-1; or you can make Sweet and Sour Sauce and Quick Hot Mustard before you start the oil.

*Venison Fondue
(Photo by
Sil Strung)*

SWEET AND SOUR SAUCE

Ingredients
1 cup (250 ml) water
½ cup (125 ml) wine vinegar
¼ cup (60 ml) soy sauce
¼ cup (60 ml) sugar
1 tablespoon butter or margarine
2 tablespoons cornstarch
3 tablespoons sherry

Cooking
1. Measure the water, wine vinegar, soy sauce, and sugar into a 2-cup (500-ml) container.
2. In a medium-size sauce pan, melt the butter over medium-high heat. Slowly add the soy sauce mixture. Simmer for 5 minutes, stirring constantly. Combine the cornstarch with the sherry and slowly add this to the pot—be careful, it might bubble up. Continue cooking for about 3–4 minutes or until it thickens. Serve hot or cold.

QUICK HOT MUSTARD

Ingredients
¼ cup (60 ml) dry mustard powder
5 teaspoons beer

Preparation
1. Place the dry mustard powder in a small Pyrex dish or serving container. Slowly add the beer, stirring constantly. Let it sit for 5 minutes—then beware! This is like the expensive Chinese hot mustard.

SAUTÉED MEDALLIONS OF ANTELOPE WITH JUNGLE JANIE'S GAME SAUCE

Sautéed Medallions of Antelope with Jungle Janie's Game Sauce (Photo by Eileen Clarke)

Yield: 2 servings

This recipe provides the easiest and tastiest way to cook and serve those tenderloin or round steak fillets. The secret to this dish is to undercook the fillets, as they will toughen quickly if overcooked. Serve it with shallots, a brown gravy, and a dash of Jungle Janie's Game Sauce.

Ingredients

6 boneless medallions of antelope
Olive oil or butter
3 shallots or green onions, finely chopped
1 cup (250 ml) beef bouillon
Freshly ground pepper
¼ cup (60 ml) Jungle Janie's Game Sauce (see following recipe)
¼ cup (60 ml) dry Marsala wine

Preparation

1. Preheat a heavy-bottomed sauté pan until it's very hot. Quickly sauté the antelope medallions in a light coating of olive oil or butter in the pan, turning to just barely brown the meat. They should look medium rare with warm red centers. Remove quickly to a serving platter and keep warm.

2. Reduce the heat to low under the saucepan. To the remainder of the drippings in the pan, add the shallots, and stir to prevent browning. Add the beef broth and Marsala to the shallots, and stir to dissolve the drippings.

3. Add Janie's Jungle Sauce or another tart lingonberry-type sauce. Stir to blend and season with pepper; the beef broth will provide the salt. Serve over rice, with a green salad.

Cutting tenderloin into medallions for Sautéed Medallions of Antelope (Photo by Eileen Clarke)

JUNGLE JANIE'S GAME SAUCE

Yield: 6 pints (3 liters)

The ultimate, secret sauce ingredient for game recipes. It is known in polite circles as Damson plum sauce.

Ingredients

10 cups (2½ liters) Damson plums (or a tart lingonberry), halved and seeded
10 cups (2½ liters) sugar
2 oranges, unpeeled and minced

Preparation

1. Wash, halve, and seed the Damson plums before measuring. Add an equal amount of sugar, and let stand for 1 hour (or up to 12 hours) to release the juices.

2. Bring the fruit mixture to a boil and simmer until the syrup is heavy and coats a large spoon. Add the minced oranges and pour at once into sterile, hot canning jars. (To sterilize jars, place in 250°F/120°C oven for 20 minutes; scald the lids in boiling water for at least 2 minutes and leave in the gently boiling water until you're ready to seal the jars. Have clean, unrusted rings ready.) Clean off the rims of the jars as you fill them and add the hot lids and rings at once. Cool on a towel.

3. Check each jar to be sure it sealed. The lid will make a popping noise and look concave when it has sealed. If you have any doubts, store in the refrigerator as you would any open jar of preserves. Sealed jars may be kept at room temperature. This is one of the best accompaniments to venison, antelope, or upland birds.

Antelope buck in morning mist (Photo by Erwin and Peggy Bauer)

COWBOY STEAKS
WITH SAWMILL GRAVY AND BANNOCK

Yield: 4 servings

The secret to cowboy steaks is deep frying. The secret to deep frying is deep fat. Forget nouvelle cuisine. This is what you need to climb that cold, nasty elk mountain all day or to sit in an Alabama tree stand in January.

Ingredients

1 cup (250 ml) flour
Salt and pepper, to taste
4 shoulder steaks, 4–6 ounces (100–175 g) each
Cooking oil or lard
1–1½ cups (250–375 ml) milk

Preparation

1. Season the flour with salt and pepper. Pound the steaks to about ¼-inch (½-cm) thickness. One at a time, cover the steaks repeatedly with flour and press it into the grain with the back of a fork.

Skinning an antelope (Photo by John Barsness)

Cooking

1. Heat about 1 inch (2½ cm) of cooking oil in the bottom of a heavy skillet to medium hot. Brown the steaks quickly, turning once, and then cover the pan, letting the steaks cook 2–3 minutes more as you would for fried chicken. Be careful to let the steaks cook to a golden brown but not burn.

2. Remove the steaks to a hot platter and pour off all but 3–4 tablespoons of the fat. Add an equal amount of flour to the pan and brown it well. Add the milk, stir over low heat until thickened, and season to taste.

BANNOCK

Yield: 4–6 servings

Here's a bit of historical trivia: Bannack, Montana, (spelled with two "a's") was the first capital of the Treasure State and only one drainage over from where Lewis and Clark's guide, Sacajawea, was finally reunited with her family. She'd been kidnapped from her Shoshone family at the headwaters of the Missouri River as a child and served as a guide mostly so she could get back home.

Richard Jackson, owner, operator, and sometimes cook of Great Divide Outfitters, insists you need a wood stove and rendered bear lard to make this traditional Native American bread, called "bannock," but he made it in my kitchen one winter's night with safflower oil and a gas range. He pronounced it a fair facsimile. But if you have a wood stove for even heat, and bear lard for taste, use it.

In the Arctic, we had bannock shaped like a pretzel. I asked our Inuit cook if there was a reason. "It cooks more evenly," Bella said; she cooks on a small propane stove. So if you have trouble with uneven cooking, poke one to four holes, evenly spaced, into the bannock once it is in the pan.

Ingredients

2 cups (500 ml) flour
2 teaspoons baking powder
½ teaspoon salt
¼ cup (60 ml) powdered milk (optional, but it makes for a lighter dough)
1 cup (250 ml) water
4–6 tablespoons lard, cooking oil, or rendered bear fat

Preparation

1. Put 1 cup (250 ml) of flour in a large mixing bowl. Add baking powder, salt, powdered milk, and water. Mix well.

2. Gradually, add the remaining 1 cup (250 ml) of flour to the bowl and stir until you have a soft, but not sticky, dough. The dough will come off the sides of the bowl as it loses its stickiness. Then pat it with the backs of your fingers, working enough flour into the dough so that it is not sticky at all. There's a balance here: working in enough flour, but not handling the dough so much that it gets tough.

3. Place dough on a floured board and pat it out to ½ inch (1 cm) thick.

Cooking

1. Heat 2–3 tablespoons of fat to medium heat in a heavy 10-inch (25-cm) skillet. When a drop of water jumps in the pan, it's ready for the bread.

2. Place the bannock gently in the pan and spread it out with your knuckles. In 8–10 minutes, tip the bannock up with a pancake turner to check it. When it is golden brown on the bottom, use the turner to slip it onto a dinner plate, and add 2–3 tablespoons more fat to the pan. Return the bannock to the pan and shake the pan back and forth to coat the bottom evenly with oil. Cook until both sides are golden brown. Serve with Cowboy Steak or at breakfast with honey or jelly.

VENISON SWISS STEAK

Venison Swiss Steak (Photo by Sil Strung)

Yield: 4 servings

A wonderful way of preparing a tougher cut of meat.

Ingredients

½ cup (125 ml) flour
½ teaspoon salt
¾ teaspoon pepper
1 tablespoon paprika
1–1½ pounds (½–¾ kg) shoulder steaks, ½ inch (1 cm) thick
3 tablespoons fat or oil
1 medium onion, chopped
¼ cup (60 ml) chopped carrots
2 cans stewed tomatoes, 14½ ounces (411 g) each

Cooking

1. Combine flour, salt, pepper, and paprika, and dredge the meat in the mixture. With a mallet or the edge of a plate, pound as much of this mixture as possible into both sides of the meat.
2. In a Dutch oven, heat the fat, and brown the meat thoroughly on both sides.
3. Add the onion, carrots, and stewed tomatoes. Cover and simmer gently until tender, about 2 hours, and serve.

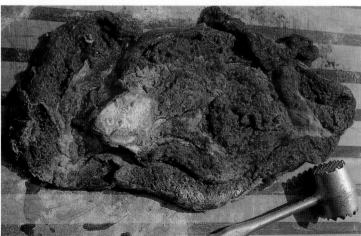

Tenderizing the meat for Venison Swiss Steak (Photo by Sil Strung)

POTSDAM STAG ROLL
WITH LINGONBERRY SAUCE

Yield: 4 servings

This is a variation on a dish served at the Ceciliahof in Potsdam, site of the Potsdam Conference following World War II. The Ceciliahof grounds include an incredible breakfast garden and remnants of the Berlin Wall that for nearly thirty years separated the castle from the river that flows below its leaded-glass windows. The lunch also included whipped cabbage, *faux* pear dumpling, and a red wine snow cone for dessert.

Pâté Filling Ingredients
1 large onion, diced
2 cloves garlic, minced
2 tablespoons butter
8 ounces (225 g) mild liver (antelope is the mildest; young deer will work)

Stag Roll Ingredients
4 steaks, 5 ounces (140 g) each, ½ inch (1 cm) thick
1 tablespoon paprika
1 tablespoon dry mustard
3–4 tablespoons flour
1–2 tablespoons oil
⅔ cup (160 ml) water

Cooking
1. On medium heat, sauté the onion and garlic in butter until lightly browned. Add the liver and continue cooking gently on medium, but not until it's tough, about 10–15 minutes. Set aside to cool.
2. When the liver is cool, run the mixture through a grinder; a food processor will work, but the grinder produces a better texture. Set the pâté filling aside.
3. Pound each steak to ¼ inch (½-cm) thickness, and cut lengthwise in half. Sprinkle each steak with ⅛–¼ teaspoon each of paprika and mustard, and spread with 1 tablespoon of pâté. Then roll, securing each steak with a toothpick.
4. Lightly flour each roll. Over medium-high heat, brown the rolls in the oil. When all sides are brown, add the water. Cover and simmer 20 minutes.
5. Serve with Lingonberry Sauce.

LINGONBERRY SAUCE

Lingonberries are a tart, reddish berry that my mother tells me were once quite common in New York. When I couldn't find any in my usual haunts, Mom tracked them down in a swishy gourmet shop near her home in Florida. Eventually, I found canned lingonberries in syrup in the Safeway in Bozeman, Montana. Go figure. If you can't find lingonberries in syrup, use whole, canned cranberries.

Ingredients
7 ounces (200 g) lingonberries in syrup
¼ cup red currant jelly
1 tablespoon Worcestershire sauce
2 tablespoons lemon juice (about ½ lemon)

Cooking
1. Combine all the ingredients in a small saucepan and bring to a gentle boil. Reduce heat to a simmer and cook 5 minutes more. Store the leftovers in the refrigerator. If you use lingonberry or cranberry jelly instead of the fruit in syrup, it will set up again once refrigerated. Either way, it's delicious reheated in the microwave, or cold over cold roast.

CITRUS POT STEAKS

Yield: 4–6 servings

Marinate, then slow cook over a cold, winter's afternoon, on the stove top—or put it in the oven while you hunt whitetails. The sherry adds a robust nutty flavor that makes tough steaks easy to come home to.

Marinade Ingredients

6 shoulder steaks, 6–8 ounces (150–225 g) each, $\frac{1}{2}$ inch (1 cm) thick
$\frac{1}{2}$ cup (125 ml) orange juice
$\frac{1}{4}$ cup (60 ml) fresh lemon juice
$\frac{1}{4}$ cup (60 ml) fresh lime juice
Salt and pepper, to taste

Cooking Ingredients

$\frac{1}{4}$ cup (60 ml) plus $\frac{1}{8}$ cup (30 ml) vegetable oil
1 large onion, sliced
3–5 cloves garlic, minced
1 large sweet bell pepper, cut in strips
1 cup (250 ml) canned corn, drained
1 cup (250 ml) beef broth
$\frac{1}{2}$ cup (125 ml) canned tomatoes, drained and chopped
$\frac{1}{2}$ cup (125 ml) dry sherry
1 bay leaf
6 medium potatoes

Preparation

1. Marinate steaks in orange, lemon, and lime juice, salt, and pepper, covered in refrigerator for 1–8 hours.

Cooking

1. Remove steaks from marinade and pat dry, reserving the juice. In a #8 Dutch oven (5-qt/ 5-liter capacity) heat $\frac{1}{4}$ cup (60 ml) oil over medium high heat, then brown the steaks one at a time, for 2–3 minutes to a side. Remove steaks.

2. Reduce to medium heat and add $\frac{1}{8}$ cup (30 ml) oil to the pan. Sauté the onion, garlic, and green pepper until tender. Add the rest of the ingredients, except the potatoes, and simmer, covered, for 45–60 minutes. Add the potatoes and continue cooking over low heat until the potatoes are tender, about 1 hour more. Alternatively, add all the ingredients at once and cook slowly in the oven at 300°F (150°C) for 2 hours.

Citrus Pot Steak (Photo by Eileen Clarke)

VENISON AND VEGETABLE PIE

Yield: 4–6 servings

A one-crust meat pie, with a creamy sauce using chunks of last year's tender venison with this summer's fresh garden vegetables. What more could you ask for?

Ingredients

1 large onion, diced

2 stalks celery, diced

$\frac{1}{2}$ green bell pepper, diced (about $\frac{1}{2}$ cup [125 ml])

2 tablespoons bacon grease or cooking oil

2 tablespoons margarine

1 pound ($\frac{1}{2}$ kg) venison, cut in 1 inch ($2\frac{1}{2}$ cm) cubes

$\frac{1}{2}$ cup (125 ml) flour

$1\frac{1}{2}$ cup (375 ml) milk

$1\frac{1}{2}$ cup (375 ml) beef bouillon

$\frac{1}{2}$ cup (125 ml) sliced fresh mushrooms

1 cup (250 ml) peas

1 cup (250 ml) sliced carrots

1 medium potato, sliced

1 tablespoon dried parsley

$\frac{1}{2}$ teaspoon paprika

$\frac{1}{2}$ teaspoon pepper, freshly ground

$\frac{1}{4}$ teaspoon salt

$\frac{1}{4}$ teaspoon celery salt

$\frac{1}{4}$ teaspoon garlic powder

Pinch of red chili flakes

Pastry Ingredients

1 cup (250 ml) flour

Dash of salt

$\frac{1}{3}$ cup (80 ml) shortening

2–4 tablespoons cold water

Cooking

1. In a #8 Dutch oven (5-qt/5-liter), sauté the onion, celery, and green pepper in the fat and margarine until limp. Push the onion, celery, and pepper to one side of the pan. Shake the meat in a bread bag in $\frac{1}{4}$ cup (60 ml) of flour and brown in the same skillet.

2. Now stir the meat and sautéed vegetables together, add the remaining $\frac{1}{4}$ cup of flour and stir. The mix will get very dry. Add the milk $\frac{1}{2}$ cup (125 ml) at a time and keep stirring; this will make your gravy. Add bouillon to thin the gravy. Now add the mushrooms, peas, carrots, potato, and seasonings. Mix thoroughly and simmer 25 minutes, covered.

3. Preheat oven to 425°F (220°C). For the top, sift together flour and salt. Cut shortening in with a pastry blender or fork, until the pieces are the size of small peas.

4. Sprinkle 1 tablespoon of water over part of the flour mixture; gently toss with a fork. Repeat until all the flour just holds together. Without a lot of excess handling, press the flour mixture into a ball and turn the ball out onto a lightly floured surface.

5. Roll out the pastry dough to $\frac{1}{8}$-inch ($\frac{1}{4}$-cm) thickness and cut into squares; lay the squares over the top of the dish (or make individual pies in ramekins) and put in the oven for 15 minutes to brown. Another option: Distribute a tube of ice-box biscuits over the top and bake as for the pie crust.

VEAL TENDERLOIN FRANÇAISE WITH HERBED POTATOES

Yield: 2–4 servings

You'll need a heavy 10-inch (25-cm) skillet, hot platter, and all the ingredients cut and measured before you start up the burner. This dish cooks up very fast.

Ingredients

1 veal tenderloin (a young doe tenderloin will do)
1 egg
$\frac{1}{4}$ cup (60 ml) flour
$\frac{1}{2}$ cup (125 ml) Parmesan cheese
$\frac{1}{4}$ cup (60 ml) butter
8–10 fresh mushrooms, halved
1 lemon
2 tablespoons dry sherry
Salt and pepper, to taste
$\frac{1}{4}$ cup (60 ml) fresh parsley, chopped

Preparation

1. Slice the tenderloin on the diagonal to $\frac{1}{8}$–$\frac{1}{4}$ inch ($\frac{1}{4}$–$\frac{1}{2}$ cm) thick. If you're using meat other than veal, slice $\frac{3}{4}$ inch (1 cm) thick, then pound with meat mallet to $\frac{1}{4}$ inch ($\frac{1}{2}$ cm), keeping a piece of plastic wrap over the meat to prevent tearing. Dry meat slices in paper towels.

2. In a shallow bowl, beat the egg and set aside; place flour in another shallow bowl and grate the Parmesan into a third.

Cooking

1. Set the frying pan on high and melt the butter, but leave only a film in the pan to cook the meat. When the butter is hot, but not smoking, dredge the meat in the flour (more to dry the meat than to coat it), then dip the meat in the egg, and coat with Parmesan. Sauté one or two at a time, 1–$1\frac{1}{2}$ minutes to a side, and place on heated platter. Test the first piece for doneness; it should be pale pink inside.

2. When you turn the last piece, add mushrooms and let them absorb the rest of the butter. Now add the sherry, lemon juice, salt, and pepper. Simmer 1 minute, then transfer the meat to the heated platter and pour the sauce over the top of the cutlets. Sprinkle with more grated cheese and the fresh parsley, and serve with Herbed Potatoes.

HERBED POTATOES

Yield: 2–4 servings

Ingredients

3 medium boiling potatoes
1 tablespoon butter or cooking oil
3–4 cloves garlic, minced
2–3 teaspoons dried sweet basil leaf
$\frac{1}{2}$ teaspoon dried thyme leaf
Salt and pepper, to taste
$\frac{1}{4}$ cup (60 ml) fresh parsley, chopped
$\frac{1}{4}$ cup (60 ml) Parmesan cheese

Preparation

1. Boil the potatoes 20–25 minutes, so they are still firm, but give to the touch. Drain, dry, and dice them into $\frac{3}{4}$ inch (1 cm) cubes.

Cooking

1. Heat butter in a heavy skillet until hot but not browning. Add potatoes and lower the heat to medium and sauté, tossing the cubes gently but frequently. Add garlic and seasonings when the potatoes begin to brown. Continue cooking until golden brown, about 15 minutes in all. Remove to serving dish, lightly toss with parsley and then grate Parmesan cheese over the top.

Whitetail bucks (Photo by Erwin and Peggy Bauer)

Venison Picatta

Yield: 3–4 servings

This is another quick-cook way of preparing a venison tenderloin—after marinating the meat in milk.

Ingredients
1½ pounds (¾ kg) venison tenderloin
1 cup (250 ml) milk
Salt and pepper, to taste
¼ cup (60 ml) flour
3 tablespoons butter
3 tablespoons olive oil
1 clove garlic, minced
¼ pound (100 g) mushrooms, sliced
½ cup (125 ml) white wine
2 tablespoons lemon juice
1 tablespoon capers, drained
¼ cup (60 ml) fresh parsley, chopped

Preparation
1. Slice the tenderloin across the grain into ½-inch (1-cm) slices. Put the slices in a non-corrosive bowl and cover with milk. Cover with plastic wrap and refrigerate for 2–8 hours.
3. Remove the meat and discard the milk mixture (or give to your faithful bird dog). Dry the tenderloin slices with a paper towel, then sprinkle them with salt and pepper and dredge in flour.

Cooking
1. In a large skillet, melt butter and olive oil over medium-high heat. When hot—but not smoking—add the meat and brown it on both sides, about 2–3 minutes.
2. Remove the meat to a warm platter. Add garlic and mushrooms to the skillet and cook for 2–3 minutes.
3. Return the venison to the skillet, adding the white wine, lemon juice, capers, and parsley. Cook over medium heat 2–3 minutes more. The mixture will begin to thicken up, so be sure to scrape the pan often.
5. Remove the meat from the pan, place on a serving platter, and pour the juices over the top.

Moose Parmesan

Yield: 4–6 servings

Tender moose is perfect for Moose Parmesan, but if you don't have any in your freezer, any young venison will work. The dish requires quite a bit of preparation, but it is one of my all-time favorites, and it can be prepared ahead of time to be heated in the oven just before dinner.

*Moose Parmesan
(Photo by
Sil Strung)*

Sauce Ingredients

1 medium onion, chopped fine
3 tablespoons olive oil
2 cloves garlic, minced
2 cans whole tomatoes, 28 ounces (795 g)
   each, puréed
¾ teaspoon oregano leaf
½ teaspoon sweet basil
¼ teaspoon thyme leaf
Salt and pepper, to taste

Meat Ingredients

1 pound (½ kg) rump steaks, sliced ½ inch
   (1 cm) thick
1 cup (250 ml) flour
1 egg, beaten
1 tablespoon basil
½ teaspoon garlic powder
½ cup (125 ml) olive oil
½ pound (250 g) provolone cheese, sliced
¼ cup (60 ml) grated Parmesan cheese

Cooking

1. In a large saucepan, brown the onion in olive oil. Add the garlic, tomatoes, and spices. Simmer for 30 minutes. While the sauce simmers, prepare the meat.

2. Pound both sides of the steaks with a tenderizing hammer to ¼-inch (½-cm) thickness. Pour ½ cup (125 ml) of the flour in a bowl. Beat the egg in a second bowl. Combine the remaining ½ cup (125 ml) of flour, the basil, and the garlic powder in a third bowl.

3. Pour the olive oil ¼ inch (½ cm) deep into a heavy skillet, and heat on medium to medium-high setting. Dip the steaks first in plain flour, then egg, then seasoned flour. You want to cook the cutlets quickly—but not burn the breading—until they're a golden brown. The sauce and meat should be done about the same time.

4. Preheat oven to 350°F (175°C). Spread a layer of tomato sauce in the bottom of an ungreased 9x13x2-inch (22x32x5-cm) baking pan. Then add a layer of the cooked meat. Cover the meat with sauce and provolone cheese. You can stop here, if you want, and put the dish in the refrigerator to cook later.

5. Place the casserole in the oven until the cheese melts and the meat is heated thoroughly (if you have put it in the refrigerator for a while, this will take 30–45 minutes). Top individual servings with a sprinkling of grated Parmesan cheese. Serve with fettucini and fried eggplant.

ROASTS AND RIBS

MUSTARD-COATED VENISON ROAST

Yield: 4–6 servings

This is a succulent way to prepare either a back, rolled, or rib roast, as the mustard coating seals in the juices. I like to do this on a spit over charcoal or on the gas barbecue. On the barbecue, a 4-pound (2-kg) roast is rare in about 1¼ hours, medium will take about 1¾ hours, and well done will take 2 hours or more. When in doubt use a meat thermometer. You can also prepare this roast recipe in the oven at 350°F (175°C).

Ingredients
1 roast, 3–5 pounds (1½–2¼ kg)
2 cloves garlic, sliced thin
Salt and pepper, to taste
1 cup (250 ml) prepared mustard

Cooking
1. Preheat propane barbecue on high for 10 minutes, then turn down to medium for cooking. If using a charcoal barbecue, start about twenty-four briquettes; when they are all white, spread them out in a single layer. You want the hot coals to sear the outside of the meat, then cool down a bit to cook the roast.

2. If you have a spit, skewer the roast; otherwise plan to cook on a grill grating. Cut small slits about 1 inch (2½ cm) deep around and throughout the meat with a paring knife and insert garlic slices. Sprinkle the roast with salt and pepper to taste.

3. With your hands or a basting brush, smear a thick coating of mustard over the roast. Place the roast over the coals and close the barbecue lid. As the roast begins to brown, baste it with the remaining mustard one more time.

Mustard-Coated Venison Roast (Photo by Sil Strung)

HONEY-GLAZED VENISON ROAST

*Mule deer buck
(Photo by Erwin
and Peggy Bauer)*

Yield: 4–6 servings

This is a quick, easy way to impress guests.

Ingredients

1 rolled shoulder roast, about 2 pounds
   (1 kg)
Salt and pepper, to taste
¾ cup (185 ml) brown sugar
¼ cup (60 ml) honey
¼ cup (60 ml) orange juice
½ cup (125 ml) water

Cooking

1. Preheat oven to 350°F (175°C). Place the roast on a rack in a small, open roasting pan. Season the meat with salt and pepper. Cook for 30 minutes.

2. Prepare the glaze. Combine the brown sugar, honey, and orange juice, and mix well. After 30 minutes, remove the roast from the oven and apply the glaze evenly on all sides. Save some of the glaze for basting during cooking. Add the water to the bottom of the pan to prevent the glaze from sticking, and return the roast to the oven.

3. Continue roasting, uncovered, basting occasionally until desired doneness, about 60–90 minutes. Test with a meat thermometer: 140°F (60°C) for rare; 160°F (70°C) for medium. Serve with pan juices over baked yams, and a green vegetable.

JOHN'S PUNK ROAST

Yield: 6–8 servings

You cooled the animal down in less than four hours, then trimmed off all the fat and gristle, but the meat still has a gamy taste? John's Punk Roast and the Cajun Venison Roast that follows are my two favorite ways to make "off" meat delicious. We've even served rutty old mule deer roasts to our non-hunting relatives and they never suspected the truth.

Above: *John's Punk Roast (Photo by Eileen Clarke)*

Right: *Inserting garlic slices into John's Punk Roast (Photo by Eileen Clarke)*

Ingredients
1 head garlic cloves for a big deer; more for larger roasts
1 rump roast

Preparation
1. Preheat oven to 300°F (150°C). Slice each garlic clove into three pieces. With a long knife, make deep slits in the roast, about 2 inches (5 cm) apart and down to the bone. If it's a boneless roast, make the slit to ½ inch (1 cm) from the bottom of the roast. Fill the holes, loosely, with garlic.

Cooking
1. Roast uncovered until the meat thermometer reads 140°F (60°C) for rare, 160°F (70°C) for medium, about 60–90 minutes. Game roasts, because of the low fat content, are best cooked only to medium well. After that they tend to get dry and tough.
2. To serve, leave the garlic in and slice as usual.

CAJUN VENISON ROAST

Yield: 6–8 servings

The Cajun roast uses the same technique as John's Punk Roast, but requires 10 more minutes to dice up a little onion and celery. If you really like the hot stuff, you can double the white, black, and cayenne peppers. This recipe is for folks who like to be able to taste the meat.

Ingredients

½ cup (125 ml) finely chopped onion
½ cup (125 ml) finely chopped celery
2 tablespoons oil
½ teaspoon Colman's English Mustard
¼ teaspoon white pepper
¼ teaspoon black pepper
2 cloves garlic, minced
¼ teaspoon cayenne
1 gamy rump roast
3 slices bacon (optional)

Preparation

1. Preheat oven to 300°F (150°C). Mix the onion, celery, oil, mustard, and seasonings in a small bowl.

2. With a long knife, make deep slits in the roast about 2 inches (5 cm) apart and down to the bone. If it's a boneless roast, cut to within ½ inch (1 cm) of the bottom of the roast.

3. Fill the pockets with the vegetable and spice mixture, saving some to rub over the top when you're done. Place the bacon over the top of the roast.

Cooking

1. Roast uncovered until the meat thermometer reads 140°F (60°C) for rare, 160°F (70°C) for medium, about 60–90 minutes.

*Whitetail buck
(Photo by Erwin
and Peggy Bauer)*

American-Style Czech Candle Roast

Yield: 6–8 servings

We were told at least eight times in twelve days that this roast, served everywhere in the Czech republic, is the Czech National Dish. It's a delightful slice of pot roast, with a delicate aromatic au jus (au jus is gravy without flour). The best candle roast we had was at the Pension Sisler in Marienske Lazne, known as Marienbad until Germany lost possession of this elegant spa town. But it was always good and always served with a flourish—along with dumplings and a side dish of red or green cabbage.

Then we went to Jenna in the region of Thuringia, former East Germany, and what should appear—the Czech National Dish—but they called it the Thuringia Regional Dish. It was just as good as the Czech National Dish. When it's not broke, I guess you don't fix it.

The American "style" here refers to using game meat. The Czechs (and Thuringians) used beef. This is a good recipe for a shoulder or any other tough roast.

Ingredients

1 roast, about 3 pounds (1½ kg)
2 tablespoons bacon fat or cooking oil
1 onion, chopped
4 carrots, diced
3 whole peppercorns
2 allspice, whole
2 juniper berries, whole
1 large bay leaf
1 cup (250 ml) water

Bugling elk during the fall rut (Photo by Sil Strung)

Cooking

1. Preheat oven to 300°F (150°C). Brown all sides of the meat in the oil on medium-high in a #8 Dutch oven or heavy roasting pan of about 5 quarts (5 liters) capacity.

2. Add the remaining ingredients, cover, and roast in the oven for 2–4 hours, until you can slice it easily. You can use a larger roast—bone-in or rolled—anything that will fit in your covered pan. A rolled shoulder roast from a forkhorn deer will take the minimum 2 hours to cook. A mature elk shoulder roast can be 100 percent larger. Just increase the other ingredients proportionately and allow for the longer cooking time.

Note: In Europe, the side dishes served with this roast included cold cabbage and carrot slaw, mashed green cabbage, and a variety of dumplings. My favorite was mashed potato shaped into a tiny pear and then fried lightly. The cook even created a false stem to complete the illusion. Our least favorite was made of mashed potato also—but molded into a ball the size of Pittsburgh and dropped in boiling salted water, then rolled in a brilliant yellow oil. I recommend red cabbage and mashed potatoes.

TOMMY'S TACOS

Mule deer buck (Photo by Erwin and Peggy Bauer)

Yield: 8–10 servings

Made with caribou gamy from the rut, or any tough or gamy-tasting meat, Tommy's Tacos is an ideal recipe to make and then sit back and watch the snow fall. Or you can start it in the morning, hunt all day, and come back to a wonderful aroma.

Ingredients
1 roast, about 4 pounds (2 kg)
1 pound (½ kg) pinto beans
4 cups (1000 ml) light beer
1 can whole tomatoes, 28 ounces (795 g), with juice
1 can diced chilies, 7 ounces (199 g)
5 cloves garlic, minced
2 tablespoons cumin seed
2 tablespoons chili powder
5 teaspoons dry oregano leaf
1 teaspoon coriander
1–1½ teaspoons cayenne
1 teaspoon salt
½ teaspoon black pepper

Cooking
1. Place everything in a covered roasting pan and cook for 7–8 hours at 250°F (120°C). Check the liquid occasionally to make sure it doesn't all cook away.
2. When the meat is done, remove it from the pot and shred with a fork. Place the shredded meat on a platter.
3. Remove half of the beans and tomatoes from the pot and chop them up in a food processor, then return to the rest of the liquid.
4. Serve the beans as a side dish, along with the pot sauce, tortillas, and usual taco fixings such as Cheddar and Monterey Jack cheese, sour cream, guacamole, lettuce, salsa, and so on.

TANGY BARBECUED ELK RIBS

Elk ribs cut down to the bone for Tangy Barbecued Elk Ribs (Photo by Sil Strung)

Yield: 4–6 servings

Most of my friends used to throw elk ribs to the dogs—until I invited them over for dinner one night. Now everyone saves their ribs for me to cook.

Tangy Barbecued Elk Ribs (Photo by Sil Strung)

Barbecue Sauce Ingredients

2 cloves garlic, minced
1 large onion, chopped
2 tablespoons butter
½ cup (125 ml) Worcestershire sauce
¼ cup (60 ml) apple cider vinegar
¼ cup (60 ml) beer
1 ¾ cup (425 ml) catsup
Tabasco sauce, to taste
Dash of cayenne
½ teaspoon dry mustard
¼ teaspoon salt
2 tablespoons brown sugar
Pinch of celery seed
Pinch of cloves
Pinch of nutmeg
Pinch of paprika

Ribs Ingredients

2–3 pounds (1–1 ½ kg) elk ribs and/or brisket
Salt and pepper, to taste
¼ cup bacon grease or cooking oil
¾ cup (250 ml) beer
½ cup (125 ml) brown sugar

Cooking

1. On low temperature in a medium-sized saucepan, sauté the garlic and onion in butter until limp. Add all of the remaining barbecue sauce ingredients and bring to a boil. Turn the heat down and simmer for 15 minutes.
2. Preheat oven to 350°F (175°C). Separate each rib. Salt and pepper the ribs to taste. Heat the bacon grease in a skillet and brown the ribs thoroughly on both sides.
3. Place ribs in a large roasting pan and cover them liberally with the barbecue sauce. Add beer and sprinkle brown sugar on top. Cover and bake for 2 ½ hours or until tender, basting frequently. Serve with sauce over mashed potatoes.

SAUERBRATEN

Yield: 6–8 servings

This recipe comes from the Strung household. Grandpa Strung's father was a chef at the famous Savoy in New York City. This is a great way of preparing any of the tougher cuts of meat like neck roasts and lower leg meat.

Marinade Ingredients

2 tablespoons salt
2 tablespoons sugar
2 cups (500 ml) apple cider vinegar
2 cups (500 ml) water
2 medium onions, sliced
1 large lemon, sliced
3 large bay leaves
10 whole peppercorns
10 whole cloves

Sauerbraten Ingredients

4 pounds (2 kg) venison meat
1/4 cup (60 ml) vegetable oil
1/2 cup (125 ml) flour
6 gingersnap cookies, crushed

Preparation

1. In a large ceramic bowl or crock, combine the salt, sugar, vinegar, water, onion, lemon slices, bay leaves, peppercorns, and cloves, and mix well.
2. Cut the meat into manageable pieces so that they will fit in a Dutch oven. Add the venison meat to the marinade and cover. Place in the refrigerator to marinate for 36 hours or more. Turn the meat occasionally.
3. Remove the meat from the marinade with a slotted spoon and pat dry with a paper towel. Set it aside. Strain the marinade, reserving all of the liquid. Discard the residue.

Cooking

1. In a large skillet, heat the vegetable oil over medium-high heat. Dust the meat in flour, then brown in the hot oil. Brown on all sides.
2. Remove the browned pieces to the Dutch oven and pour the strained marinade over the meat, cover, and simmer gently for 2–3 hours. This cooking time depends upon the cut of meat used.
3. When the meat is tender, remove from the pot and cut into thick slices. Thicken the pan juices with 6 gingersnap cookies. If you don't like the flavor of ginger, you can use 2 tablespoons flour in a little cold water. Pour thickened pan juices over meat and serve with potato dumplings, red cabbage, dark bread, and a good beer.

Elk cow and bull (Photo by Eileen Clarke)

VENISON ASADO

Yield: 6–8 servings

Asado is Spanish for "roast." I learned this recipe on one of my many stays in Mexico. There are quite a few steps to the recipe but the meal is well worth it, and it can be prepared ahead of time and reheated just before serving.

Ingredients

1 rump roast, about 3–4 pounds (1½–2 kg)

1 head garlic, peeled but left whole

1 medium onion, thinly sliced

1½ tablespoons garlic salt

1 teaspoon salt

1 cube beef bouillon

10 medium-sized whole tomatoes

Freshly ground pepper to taste

8–10 potatoes

½ head of lettuce, shredded

1 red onion, thinly sliced

1 lime

½ cup (125 ml) vegetable oil

½ pound (250 g) feta cheese, crumbled, or Monterey Jack or Gouda cheese, coarsely grated

Elk bull in Yellowstone National Park (Photo by Erwin and Peggy Bauer)

Cooking

1. Place the rump roast in a large soup pot and cover with water. Add the garlic, onion, garlic salt, salt, and beef bouillon cube, and bring to a rapid boil. Reduce the heat, cover, and simmer gently for 2–3 hours until the meat falls from the bone.

2. Remove the meat from the pot and set aside to cool. Add the tomatoes to the pot and cook until soft. Mash the tomatoes in the liquid and season with the pepper. Keep warm. This is the au jus. Dice the cooled meat into 1-inch (2½-cm) cubes. Set aside.

3. In the meantime, boil the potatoes until you can just barely stick a fork into them. Remove from heat, drain, and set aside to cool. When cool, remove the skin and dice into 1-inch (2½-cm) pieces and set aside. Place the lettuce and red onion on a plate and squeeze lime juice over the top. Let sit for 20 minutes.

4. In a large, heavy skillet heat ½ cup (125 ml) vegetable oil. When the oil is hot but not smoking add the cubed meat and potatoes and brown thoroughly.

5. To serve, spoon some of the meat and potato mixture on a plate; spread the lettuce and red onion over it, pour some of the au jus over that, and top it off with the cheese.

VENISON AU JUS

Yield: 4–6 servings

I use a 2½-quart (2-liter) crock pot and set the meal up the night before. This allows me a day of hunting or fishing, and dinner is ready on my return.

Ingredients
2 cans beef consommé, 10½ ounces (298 g) each
½ cup water
1 envelope Italian dressing mix, 6 ounces (170 g)
1 venison shoulder roast, about 2 pounds (1 kg)
6 deli steak rolls

Cooking
1. Place the consommé, water, and Italian dressing mix in a crock pot and stir well. Add the meat. Set the crock pot on low and cover. Cook all night and the following day.
2. When you come back from fishing, just shred the meat and pile it liberally on deli steak rolls. Pour off the juice in the crock pot, putting some directly on the sandwich meat, and the rest in a bowl for dipping. Serve with a tossed salad.

Venison Au Jus (Photo by Sil Strung)

ORGAN MEATS

OVEN-BAKED STUFFED VENISON HEART

Yield: 2–3 servings

A lot of people shudder at the thought of eating liver and heart. I think heart has a wonderful flavor, and this recipe proves it.

Ingredients
1 venison heart, whole
2 tablespoons butter
1 tablespoon chopped onion
3 tablespoons chopped celery
1 ½ cups (375 ml) bread, dried and cubed
¼ teaspoon parsley, dried
Pinch of ground thyme
Pinch of garlic powder
Pinch of oregano powder
Salt and pepper, to taste
1 cup (250 ml) beef bouillon
2 slices bacon

Buggling elk bull (Photo by Sil Strung)

Preparation
1. Preheat oven to 325°F (190°C).
2. Cut the heart open by placing the knife blade parallel to the cutting board and slicing one third of the way into the heart, as with pita bread. Clean by removing the veins and arteries. Rinse with water.

Cooking
1. Heat the butter in a heavy skillet over medium heat. When melted, add the onions and celery, and sauté until translucent, about 2 minutes. Add the bread to the pan and remove from heat. The heavy skillet will keep things warm.
2. Season the mixture with parsley, thyme, garlic, oregano, salt, and pepper. Stir the stuffing a few times to blend in the spices. Stuff the heart with this mixture and truss with toothpicks or turkey skewers.
3. Place the heart in a small roasting pan and pour the bouillon around it. Wrap the bacon slices around the heart.
4. Cover and bake in the oven until fork tender, about 1 ½–2 hours. The heart will come out very dark. Serve with the pan juices poured over the heart, mashed or boiled potatoes, and salad.

VENISON LIVER AND ONIONS

Yield: 2–4 servings

In my opinion, there's nothing like the taste of fresh liver. Those of you with like minds should always carry a plastic bag or two in your hunting jackets for use in the safe, clean transport of this organ. While antelope is the mildest of all venison liver, I have found that soaking any liver in cold water overnight, before freezing, will greatly enhance its flavor.

Ingredients
1 pound (½ kg) venison liver
¼ cup (60 ml) flour
8 slices bacon
3 tablespoons bacon grease
3 tablespoons butter
1 cup (250 ml) sliced onions

Cooking
1. Place the liver on a cutting board; remove any hardened skin or veins. Then, holding the knife blade parallel to the cutting board, cut across the liver, creating ½-inch (1-cm) thick steaks. Dry the liver with paper towels, then dredge in flour, and set aside.
2. Cook the bacon over medium heat in a heavy iron skillet until cooked, about 5 minutes. Remove the bacon strips and set them aside on a warm platter. Reserve about 3 tablespoons of the bacon grease.
3. Add butter to the reserved grease and set on medium heat. Add the onions and sauté until tender, about 5 minutes. Remove the onions, drain, and place on a platter with the bacon.
4. Place the liver in the skillet and cook over medium heat until blood comes to the top. Turn the meat over, return the cooked onions and bacon to the pan, and continue cooking for 1–2 minutes. The liver should be on the pink side. Be careful not to overcook as this will toughen it.

SCRAPPLE

Yield: 4–6 servings

When a deer is brought into camp, tradition demands that scrapple be served that night. Scrapple is also excellent for breakfast, served with eggs.

Ingredients
4 cups (1000 ml) beef bouillon
1 cup (250 ml) corn meal
1 teaspoon salt
½ cup (125 ml), plus 3 tablespoons, butter
  or margarine
1½ pounds (¾ kg) venison liver, finely
  chopped
½ pound (250 g) venison heart, finely
  chopped
1 onion, finely chopped
½ cup (125 ml) flour

Cooking
1. Measure the beef bouillon, cornmeal, and salt into a large saucepan and bring to a boil, stirring constantly. Reduce heat, cover, and simmer slowly until the mixture is difficult to stir. Set aside.
2. In a heavy skillet, melt ½ cup (125 ml) butter and fry the liver, heart, and onions, stirring frequently, until the meat is an even brown color, about 5–7 minutes. Stir this into the cooked cornmeal.
3. Pour the mixture into an 9x13x2-inch (22x32x5-cm) baking pan, set aside to cool for 2–3 hours; the scrapple will firm up as it cools.
4. To serve, slice the scrapple into ¼-inch (½-cm) slices, dredge in flour, and fry in the remaining 3 tablespoons of butter until both sides are golden brown.

TOUGHER CUTS: BURGERS AND STEW MEATS

VENISON BURGER

It's easier to describe what burger isn't than what it is. It isn't the tender chunks of meat that you make into roasts and steaks. It isn't the sinewy lower leg meat you make into stew. It's the in-betweens: what isn't big enough for a steak after trimming and what's left on the bones after butchering. Gather up those nameless chunks and trim them carefully.

If you are fortunate to have lots of game meat, and love the variety of dishes you can make with ground venison, dedicate a shoulder to the grinder. If you're like me, the burger is what you search for—like the classic diving duck—in the bottom of the freezer.

Note: Whichever recipe you use, remember that once you add fat, you limit the freezer life of the package. One way to beat that factor is to grind up only as much burger as you'll eat in six months. That's the freezer life of fat. I've kept fat-free meat in my chest freezers, without freezer burn, for as long as eight years.

The other factor that limits freezer life is how much of the surface of the meat is exposed. Burger, by definition, is high in surface exposure. That's a second reason to grind a small amount at a time. Wrap what you're not going to grind right away into large packages, clearly marked "For Burger." Then, come June, you won't have to do the diving duck routine.

Here are three recipes from three different households.

MOO BURGER

Ingredients
5 pounds (2¼ kg) venison scraps
5 pounds (2¼ kg) cheap beef burger (the fattiest kind)

Preparation and Cooking
1. Our neighbors up the road, Jay and Bev Rightnour, prefer the richer taste of beef added to their burger. So they go Sil one step further: they add beef burger fifty-fifty to their ground venison.

SLIM BURGER

This is the easiest recipe of all, but it's not for people who barbecue burgers.

Ingredients
Venison, any amount, trimmed and de-fatted

Preparation and Cooking
1. After trimming the meat carefully of all fat and wiping off all hair and other debris, run it once through a meat grinder (food processors work, but grinders leave a better texture). Once is enough, but if you feel you haven't done enough work yet, grind the meat again, then double wrap tightly and freeze.
2. To cook, add a small amount of cooking oil or sprinkle granular garlic powder on the pan to keep the meat from sticking.

Sil's Burger

Ingredients

5 pounds (2 $\frac{1}{4}$ kg) venison

1 $\frac{1}{2}$ pounds ($\frac{3}{4}$ kg) beef suet from the butcher

3–5 cloves garlic, minced, or more to taste

Preparation and Cooking

1. Sil barbecues a lot, and venison without fat won't hold together on the grill. She trims, wipes, and grinds just like with Slim Burger, but adds the beef suet on the first grind, a little at a time, then adds the garlic when she grinds it the second time.

Venison Patties with Mushroom Gravy

Yield: 4 servings

This is a different way of serving venison burger that goes great with mashed potatoes and string beans.

Ingredients

2 tablespoons butter

$\frac{1}{4}$ pound (100 g) mushrooms, sliced

2 tablespoons chopped onions

2 tablespoons flour

2 cups (500 ml) beef bouillon

$\frac{1}{4}$ teaspoon salt

$\frac{1}{8}$ teaspoon pepper

$\frac{1}{8}$ teaspoon nutmeg

Salt and pepper, to taste

1 pound ($\frac{1}{2}$ kg) Sil Burger or Moo Burger made into patties

$\frac{1}{2}$ cup (125 ml) whipping cream

$\frac{1}{2}$ teaspoon parsley

Cooking

1. In a medium-sized sauce pan, melt the butter. Add the mushrooms and onions, and sauté over medium heat for 5 minutes until the mushrooms are limp and the onions translucent. Add the flour to the pan and blend. Slowly pour in the bouillon. Cook and stir until slightly thickened, about 5 minutes. Season with the salt, pepper, and nutmeg. Keep warm on the burner.

2. Salt and pepper the patties and fry over medium heat to desired doneness. Remove to a warm platter and add the mushroom sauce to the skillet, scraping the burger juices into the mushroom sauce. Slowly pour in the cream, and heat but do not bring to a boil as the cream will curdle. Pour this sauce over the burgers and garnish with parsley.

Mule deer buck at the end of the rut (Photo by Erwin and Peggy Bauer)

MEAT LOAF

Yield: 4–6 servings

Save your gamy burger for Cajun Breakfast Sausage or Jerky. Use Slim Burger from a sweet tasting animal for the Meat Loaf. And don't forget to make enough for sandwiches: Meat Loaf sandwiches in the woods are better than caviar in the city.

Ingredients

1½ pounds (¾ kg) Slim Burger
½ pound (250 g) Easy Breakfast Sausage, or any breakfast sausage
¼ cup (60 ml) bread crumbs
1 egg, slightly beaten
¼ cup (60 ml) catsup
Dash of oregano
¼ teaspoon pepper, freshly ground
¼ teaspoon garlic powder
½ teaspoon lemon peel, freshly grated
¼ cup (60 ml) onion, chopped
1 can seasoned tomato sauce, 8 ounces (227 g)
2 large potatoes, cut in long strips, ½ inch (1 cm) thick

Cooking

1. Preheat oven to 350°F (175°C). In a large mixing bowl, combine burger, sausage, bread crumbs, egg, catsup, and seasonings. Mix well with your hands. Place the meat mixture in a greased 8x11-inch (20x27-cm) baking dish, leaving a ½-inch (1-cm) space around the meat. Pour the tomato sauce over the top, and surround the meat with the potato strips.

2. Bake for 90 minutes until well done. Remove from the oven and drain or spoon off any excess fat. Let the meat sit for 10 minutes; it will firm up and make slicing much easier. Serve with salad and peas.

EASY BREAKFAST SAUSAGE

Yield: 1 pound (½ kg) feeds 2–4

For a hearty hunting breakfast, when the weather's cold or wet—or both—cook up some sausage and bannock. That might, all by itself, be a complete protein, but you'd better add coffee for nutritional balance.

Make these sausages with Slim Burger and you'll be healthier, but you won't have any drippings in the pan. If you want lots of drippings to make Sawmill Gravy, use Sil Burger or Moo Burger. As with burger, make up only as much sausage as you'll use in six months.

Side pork comes from the lower rib cage of the pig and is usually smoked for bacon or salted for salt pork. I use it for sausage to have a low-sodium breakfast meat.

Ingredients

4 pounds (2 kg) ground venison
¾ pound (350 g) side pork, in 2-inch (5-cm) chunks
3½ teaspoons ground sage
2½ teaspoons pepper
1 teaspoon salt

Preparation

1. Run all the meat through the grinder once, adding side pork to each pound of burger as you go.

2. In a large pan, add the spices and work them in with your hands. Double wrap tightly and freeze.

3. To cook, shape into patties and fry or broil.

EASY CAJUN SAUSAGE

Yield: 1 pound (½ kg) feeds 2–4

The spices in Cajun Sausage mask strong gamy flavors, and it's just as easy to make as the recipe for Easy Breakfast Sausage.

*Easy Cajun Sausage
(Photo by
Eileen Clarke)*

Ingredients

4 pounds (2 kg) venison burger

¾ pound (350 g) side pork, in 2-inch (5-cm) chunks

1 cup (250 ml) finely chopped onions

8 cloves crushed garlic

1 tablespoon crushed hot peppers, or to taste

2 teaspoons cayenne, or to taste

2 teaspoons pepper

1 teaspoon allspice

1 cup (250 ml) chopped parsley

Preparation

1. Run all the meat through the grinder once, adding side pork to each pound of burger as you go.

2. In a large pan, add the spices and parsley to the meat, and work them in with your hands. Double wrap tightly and freeze.

3. To cook, shape into patties and fry or broil.

North Country Chili

Yield: 6–8 servings

Before you even dip into the pot, take out 3 cups (750 ml) of finished chili and set it aside in the refrigerator. Then, some night when you're tired and need a quick, delicious dinner, retrieve your precious 3 cups (750 ml) of chili and make the Chili Cheese Bake that follows this recipe.

North Country Chili (Photo by Eileen Clarke)

Ingredients

3 ounces (84 g) tomato paste
4 cups (1000 ml) canned or fresh tomatoes, coarsely chopped
5 cups (1250 ml) beef broth
1 cup (250 ml) red wine
$\frac{1}{4}$ cup (60 ml) apple cider vinegar
2 teaspoons chili pepper
2 teaspoons ground cumin

1 teaspoon ground oregano
$\frac{1}{2}$ teaspoon black pepper
3 tablespoons oil
2 pounds (1 kg) burger
2 large onions, coarsely chopped
1 head of garlic, minced
1 bell pepper, coarsely chopped
4 cups (1000 ml) kidney beans, fully cooked
2 cups (500 ml) corn

Cooking

1. In a heavy-bottomed pot (6-qt/5$\frac{1}{2}$-liter capacity minimum) combine the tomato paste, tomatoes, broth, red wine, apple cider vinegar, and spices. Bring to a slow boil.

2. In a large skillet, heat 1$\frac{1}{2}$ tablespoons of oil and brown the meat quickly in two or three batches. Add browned meat to the soup pot as it's done.

3. Add more oil to the pan, so there's a total of 2 tablespoons, and add the onions, garlic, and bell pepper, stirring until they are light brown. Add them to the soup pot.

4. Cover and simmer gently for 1$\frac{1}{2}$ hours. Add the beans and corn, and bring back up to a gentle boil, stirring occasionally. Serve.

CHILI CHEESE BAKE

Yield: 4 servings

This dish is so easy you can put it together faster than I can explain it.

Chili Cheese Bake (Photo by Eileen Clarke)

Ingredients

3 cups (750 ml) leftover North Country Chili

1 16 ounces (454 g) container of cottage cheese

1½ cups (375 ml) medium or sharp Cheddar cheese, grated

Cooking

1. In a deep 1½-qt (1½-liter) casserole combine the chili and cottage cheese.

2. Spread the grated cheese on top and bake at 350°F (175°C) for 1 hour until the cheese is melted and chili is bubbling. Then place directly under the broiler to brown the cheese, 5–8 minutes.

Variation: Brown 6 corn tortillas in light oil, or toast them in the toaster, and tear them into 2-inch (5-cm) strips to line the bottom of the dish. Proceed as above.

SLOW COOK SPAGHETTI SAUCE

Yield: 6–8 servings

When I make spaghetti I like to make it in large quantities. Spaghetti sauce freezes up nicely. At first I used Tupperware products, but the sauce discolored the containers. Instead, I save 2-liter plastic jugs from either Pepsi or Coke (I am not partial). This way I can defrost the sauce in the container in the sink, and then recycle the container.

Ingredients

2 cloves garlic, minced
$\frac{1}{4}$ onion, chopped
3 tablespoons olive oil
1 pound ($\frac{1}{2}$ kg) hot Italian sausage, sliced in
    three equal parts
1 pound ($\frac{1}{2}$ kg) venison burger
2 cans ready cut peeled tomatoes, 28 ounces
    (795 g) each, with liquid
1 can tomato purée, 10$\frac{3}{4}$ ounces (305 g)
2 cans tomato paste, 6 ounces (170 g) each
3$\frac{1}{2}$ cups (875 ml) water
$\frac{1}{2}$ teaspoon sugar
1 tablespoon leaf oregano
1 tablespoon basil leaves
2 teaspoons parsley
$\frac{1}{2}$ teaspoon leaf marjoram
$\frac{1}{2}$ teaspoon fennel
$\frac{1}{4}$ teaspoon whole thyme
$\frac{1}{4}$ teaspoon rosemary
$\frac{1}{4}$ teaspoon salt
$\frac{1}{4}$ teaspoon pepper
$\frac{1}{8}$ teaspoon powdered sage
1 bay leaf

Cooking

1. In a heavy skillet, sauté the garlic and onion in olive oil until translucent. Remove with a slotted spoon to a large, 8–10-quart (7$\frac{1}{2}$–9$\frac{1}{2}$-liter) sauce pan. Brown the sausage, then the burger, and add this to the sauce pan.

2. Add the cans of whole tomatoes, tomato purée, tomato paste, and water, and stir to mix. Now add the sugar and seasonings. Cook over low heat for 3–4 hours, stirring occasionally. Serve over hot spaghetti.

QUICK COOK SPAGHETTI SAUCE

Yield: 4–6 servings

Seven ingredients—eight, if you count the pasta. Thirty minutes. You could make a PB and J sandwich faster but you wouldn't have leftovers.

Ingredients

1 pound (½ kg) Slim Burger
2 tablespoons oil
1 large onion, coarsely chopped
4–6 large cloves garlic, minced
1½ tablespoons sweet basil
¼ teaspoon white pepper
1 can whole tomatoes, 28 ounces (795 g)

Cooking

1. In a #8 Dutch oven or heavy-bottomed 5-qt. (4.75-liter) pan, brown the burger in medium-hot oil. Then push it to one side of the pan and sauté the onions and garlic until tender. Add the basil and white pepper. Stir the spices into the burger and onion until the heat releases their aroma.

2. Drain the tomato juice into the pot, quarter the tomatoes, and add them. Simmer uncovered while you start the water for pasta. By the time the spaghetti is ready, the sauce will have lost just a bit of liquid and be ready for the table.

Quick Cook Spaghetti Sauce (Photo by Eileen Clarke)

Montana Creole Pie

Yield: 6–8 servings

I've tried those New Orleans recipes, and even my friend Milo, who lost his sense of taste and smell in Vietnam, can taste those. While it's still pretty spicy, this is a three-decker meat pie for more moderate tastes, and it's a good recipe for rank venison burger, whether you added fat or not.

First Layer Ingredients

2 pounds (1 kg) ground venison
2 eggs, lightly beaten
¾ cup (185 ml) bread crumbs
2 tablespoons butter
1 cup (250 ml) finely chopped onion
1 cup (250 ml) finely chopped celery
¾ cup (185 ml) finely chopped bell pepper
2 teaspoons Worcestershire sauce
¼ teaspoon Tabasco sauce
4 cloves garlic, minced
½ teaspoon cayenne
½ teaspoon pepper
1¼ teaspoons white pepper
¾ teaspoon ground cumin
¾ teaspoon dried thyme
¼ cup or 2 ounces (60 ml) evaporated milk (open a 5-ounce (150-ml) can; you'll use the rest for the potato layer)

Second and Third Layers Ingredients

1½ pounds (¾ kg) potatoes
1 cup (250 ml) diced carrots, diced to ½-inch (1-cm) chunks
1 cup (250 ml) frozen peas
1 cup (250 ml) frozen corn
¼ cup (60 ml) pan drippings; supplement with about 1 tablespoon oil if you used unfatted burger
1 cup (250 ml) coarsely chopped onion
¼ teaspoon white pepper
¼ teaspoon garlic powder (not garlic salt)
¼ teaspoon onion powder
Pinch of cayenne
1 tablespoon butter
3 ounces (90 ml) evaporated milk

First Layer Preparation and Cooking

1. Combine ground meat, eggs, and bread crumbs in a 9x13-inch (22x32-cm) roasting pan. Set aside.
2. Melt the butter in a small saucepan. Add the vegetables, Worcestershire and Tabasco sauces, garlic, and seasonings, and cook over high heat, stirring constantly, for about 4 minutes. Cool until you can work mixture with your fingers.
3. Preheat oven to 450°F (230°C). Add the vegetables and the evaporated milk to the meat. Shape it into a flat loaf, leaving a 1-inch (2½-cm) margin all around the edge of the pan.
4. Bake for 30 minutes, until brown. Pour off pan drippings, and reserve 3 tablespoons of drippings for the next layer.

Second and Third Layers Preparation and Cooking

1. Boil the potatoes until fork tender.
2. While the potatoes are boiling, microwave or steam the carrots, peas, and corn until they're bright in color. (They'll only be cooked another 5 minutes total, so be sure they're nearly ready to eat.) Heat the drippings and oil in a large skillet, then add the carrots, peas, corn, onion, and seasonings, and sauté 4–5 minutes, stirring often. Remove from heat.
3. Mash the potatoes, adding 1 tablespoon of butter and 3 ounces (90 ml) of evaporated milk. Whip until creamy, adding some of the cooking water if needed.
4. Pour the corn and pea mixture on top of the meat, being careful to keep it from the edges. Now layer the potatoes over the top, patting it evenly with your hands and sealing all the vegetables in.
5. Set under the broiler, and brown the top, approximately 8–10 minutes at 525°F (275°C).

MEXICAN FIESTA CASSEROLE

Yield: 4–6 servings

You can assemble the Fiesta Casserole ahead of time, refrigerate, and then bake just before dinner. And if there are any leftovers, they're great the next day, too.

Ingredients

1 pound (½ kg) ground venison
Salt and pepper, to taste
1 cup (250 ml) sour cream
⅔ cup (160 ml) mayonnaise
1 cup (250 ml) grated sharp Cheddar cheese
2 tablespoons chopped onion
1 jalapeño pepper, minced
¾ cup (185 ml) chopped sweet green
    peppers
2 tomatoes, thinly sliced
¼ teaspoon paprika

Crust Ingredients

2 cups (500 ml) flour
1 tablespoon baking powder
½ teaspoon salt
¼ cup (60 ml) shortening
¾ cup (185 ml) milk

Cooking

1. Season the burger with salt and pepper, and brown in a heavy skillet. Drain and set aside. Mix sour cream, mayonnaise, cheese, and onion, and set that aside. Combine the jalapeño and sweet peppers.

2. Pour flour, baking powder, and salt into a bowl and mix thoroughly with a fork. Cut in the shortening with a pastry blender. The mixture will look like coarse crumbs.

3. Make a well in the flour mixture. Add the milk and stir rapidly with a fork. The dough will be sticky. Remove from the bowl and pat the dough into a greased 9x13x2-inch (22x32x5-cm) pan. Press the dough ½ inch (1 cm) up the sides. (Alternatively, make up 2 cups (456 g) Bisquick.)

4. Preheat oven to 375°F (190°C). Layer meat, tomatoes, peppers; spoon the sour cream mixture over the top and sprinkle with paprika. Bake for 25–30 minutes. Casserole is done when the sour cream turns a light golden brown.

Bighorn ram (Photo by John Barsness)

Tangy Venison Stew

Yield: 4–6 servings

I use a #8 Dutch oven (5-quart/4¾-liter capacity), which gives me the option of cooking on the stove top or just setting the dish in a 300°F (150°C) oven. The cast-iron of the Dutch oven also provides a certain amount of iron to the diet. You can use a soup pot, too, if it has a heavy bottom.

Ingredients

2 pounds (1 kg) stew meat
2 cups (500 ml) beef stock or broth
6 whole cloves
2 teaspoon thyme
2 tablespoons mustard
¼ cup malt vinegar
1 cup (250 ml) tomato sauce
Salt and pepper, to taste
8 medium potatoes
1 tablespoon plus 1 tablespoon cooking oil
4 medium onions, coarsely chopped
4–6 cloves garlic, minced

Preparation

1. Cut stew meat into cubes. I like large pieces—about 2-inch (5-cm) squares. Then dry the meat with paper towels so it will brown well.
2. Measure the broth into a bowl. Chop up the cloves a bit and add along with thyme, mustard, malt vinegar, tomato sauce, salt, and pepper.

Cooking

1. Put the broth and herb mixture into a Dutch oven and turn on medium heat. In a separate pot, put the potatoes on to boil.
2. In 1 tablespoon of oil, brown the meat in a heavy-bottom skillet a few pieces at a time and put into Dutch oven to keep warm as you work.
3. When all the meat is browned, put 1 tablespoon oil into the skillet and gently sauté the onion and garlic until just soft. Add the onions to the broth and meat mixture.
4. Bring the mixture to a slow simmer, then cover and keep at a slow simmer for 45–90 minutes, depending on the toughness of the meat. The sauce should be thick. If not, thicken with either 1 tablespoon corn starch or finely grate one potato into the pot. The potato will thicken the sauce as quickly as the corn starch, and will not add any empty calories.
3. When the meat is tender, cut the boiled potatoes into 2-inch (5-cm) cubes and add to the stew. Heat thoroughly and serve.

Caribou in Denali National Park, Alaska (Photo by Erwin and Peggy Bauer)

HEARTY FALL SOUP

Yield: 4–6 servings

This is a quicker version of Sauerbraten, heavily spiced, and good for stew meat that has a bit too much of its own flavors.

Ingredients

2 pounds (1 kg) stew meat
3 slices bacon
1½ cups (375 ml) unsweetened apple sauce
¾ cup (185 ml) red wine vinegar
2 teaspoons fresh ginger, grated
1 cinnamon stick, about 3 inches (7½ cm) long
2 bay leaves
1 large onion
3 cloves, stuck into the onion
1 tablespoon bacon grease
1 tablespoon cooking oil
2 lemons

Preparation

1. Cut the stew meat into 1½-inch (3½-cm) cubes and dry on paper towels. In a heavy skillet, brown the bacon and set aside to cool.
2. In a #8 Dutch oven (5-qt/4¾-liter pot) mix the apple sauce and red wine vinegar, then add ginger, cinnamon stick, bay leaves, and the large onion with three cloves stuck into it. (It makes the cloves easier to retrieve when you're ready to serve.)

Cooking

1. Pour off all but 1 tablespoon of the bacon grease and add an additional 1 tablespoon cooking oil. Bring this to a moderately high heat and brown the meat a few pieces at a time. Keep adding browned meat to the Dutch oven, then when all meat is browned, bring the entire pot to a boil, cover, and reduce the heat. Simmer 45–90 minutes, until the meat is fork tender. Remove all three cloves from the onion. (Optional: You can also remove the cinnamon stick and bay leaves before serving. If you have leftovers, you can return them to the pot to develop more flavor overnight.)
2. To serve, squeeze 2–3 teaspoons of lemon juice and grate some lemon rind over each serving.

Hearty Fall Soup (Photo by Eileen Clarke)

BURGUNDY BEAR

Yield: 3–4 servings

This recipe is another good reason for having a bottle of Burgundy in the house. This makes a great Dutch-oven meal.

Above: *Black bear (Photo by Erwin and Peggy Bauer)*

Right: *Burgundy Bear (Photo by Sil Strung)*

Ingredients

¼ cup (60 ml) flour
¼ teaspoon salt
¼ teaspoon pepper
1 pound (½ kg) bear meat, cubed
2 tablespoons vegetable oil
2 tablespoons butter
1 cup (250 ml) beef broth

1½ cups (375 ml) Burgundy wine
1 tablespoon parsley
Pinch of allspice
Pinch of thyme leaf
½ teaspoon garlic grains (a granulated garlic powder)
2 carrots, cut into chunks
1 medium onion, sliced thin

Cooking

1. Combine flour, salt, and pepper in a small bag and shake well to blend. Add the bear meat and shake to coat the meat.

2. In a Dutch oven, heat the oil and butter over medium-high heat and brown the meat evenly on all sides. Reduce to low, and add the broth, wine, and seasonings. Place carrots and onions in the pot.

3. Cover and cook over low heat for 1 hour or until the meat is tender. Serve over buttered noodles.

Black bear (Photo by Erwin and Peggy Bauer)

TRADITIONAL JERKY

Yield: 1 pound (½ kg) feeds 3 people

Jerky is a high-energy food that weighs little in your hunting pack. Take it along fishing, too. This recipe uses strips of venison—deer, antelope, billy goat, or musk ox—anything will do. We store it in coffee cans to keep the mice from feasting.

Ingredients

4 pounds (2 kg) venison
2 teaspoons salt, or to taste
1 tablespoon paprika
¼ teaspoon powdered cloves
½ teaspoon nutmeg
½ teaspoon celery salt
½ teaspoon pepper
1 teaspoon cayenne
1 teaspoon curry powder

Preparation

1. Slice the venison into 2x8-inch (5x20-cm) strips, ¼ inch (½ cm) thick. Cut away all fat and gristle from the meat. Combine seasonings in a shaker.
2. Pound the meat with a meat mallet and, as you pound, generously sprinkle with the seasonings.

Cooking

1. Place the strips directly on the oven rack, heat the oven to 150°F (65°C), and leave until all the moisture is gone, usually about 7–12 hours. The strips should be dry as leather, but supple enough to bend without breaking.

*Whitetail buck
(Photo by Erwin
and Peggy Bauer)*

BURGER JERKY

Yield: 1 pound (½ kg) feeds 3 people

Here's a variation on Traditional Jerky: It's easier on the teeth, and has no nitrates or food coloring. Some might think it's not the real stuff, but it's less work and I prefer the texture.

Burger Jerky (Photo by Eileen Clarke)

Ingredients

For each 1 pound (½ kg) of slim burger add:
½ teaspoon salt
½ teaspoon garlic powder
2 teaspoons onion powder
2 teaspoons ground oregano
½ teaspoon white pepper
¼ teaspoon dried red chili peppers, crushed

Preparation

1. Put all the ingredients in a large bowl and mix well. Refrigerate for 12–24 hours.
2. Line a standard 10x15-inch (25x37-cm) cookie sheet with wax paper. With your fingers, press the meat out on the cookie sheet, ¼ inch (½ cm) thick. (If you need to use a rolling pin to get the meat that thin, first press it to the shape of the cookie sheet with your fingers, then lift out with the waxed paper and roll. Return to the cookie sheet.) Put the pressed meat in the freezer until you can just cut it easily. My chest freezer, on its coldest setting, takes about 90 minutes.
3. Lift the partly frozen meat off the cookie sheet with the wax paper and place it on a cutting board, paper side up. Peel the wax paper off. Now cut the meat into strips about 1x6 inches (2½ x15 cm) in size and lay the pieces on a shelf in the middle of the oven.

Cooking

1. Cook slowly at 160°F (70°C) for 6–8 hours. Put a cookie sheet under it if you want, but it won't fall through.
2. When the jerky is totally dry, dump it into a gauze bag—a good use for game bags—and hang it in a cool, dry place for 24–48 hours. That will ensure that all the moisture is out. Then bag it in resealable bags and enjoy.

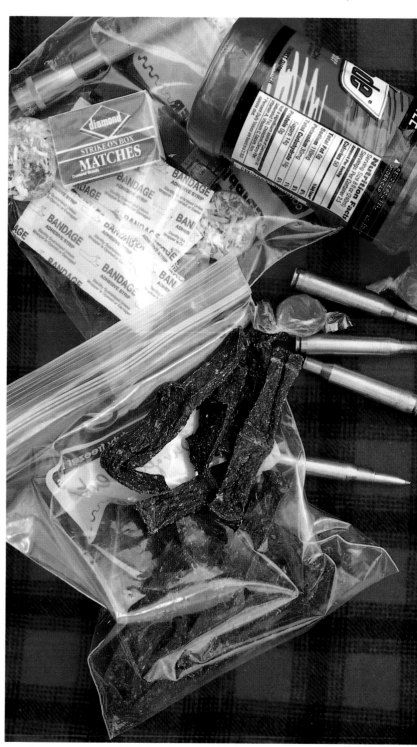

TRADITIONAL CORNED VENISON

Yield: 2–4 servings per 1 pound (½ kg) venison

If you've got a spare refrigerator in the basement (for beer or bear), this is the time to use it. Or, just put the crock in an unheated basement. You need a constant temperature of 45°F (7°C) or below—but not below freezing—for the two weeks of corning.

    This recipe will work best with brisket, but a boned-out neck roast or shoulder roast also works well.

Corned Venison prior to stewing (Photo by Sil Strung)

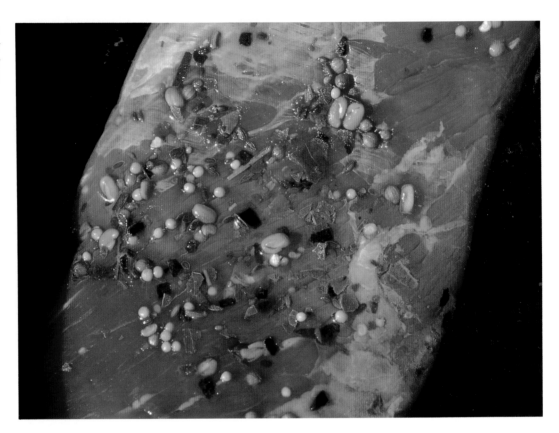

Corning Ingredients

4 quarts (4 liters) water
3 tablespoons brown sugar
3 cloves garlic, minced
2 cups (500 ml) salt
1 teaspoon peppercorns
1 teaspoon coriander
¼ teaspoon allspice
¼ teaspoon mustard seed
⅛ teaspoon ginger
1 cinnamon stick, about 2 inches (5 cm) long
10 whole cloves
1 bay leaf
1 dried red chili, crushed
6–8 pounds (2 ¾–3 ½ kg) venison meat

Cooking Ingredients

3 pounds (1 ½ kg) corned meat
3 onions, sliced
3 cloves garlic, minced
6 whole cloves
2 bay leaves
4 medium potatoes
8 medium carrots
1 small head cabbage, cut into even-sized
   wedges

Traditional Corned Venison (Photo by Sil Strung)

Preparation

1. Pour all the liquid, sugar, garlic, and seasonings into a 3-gallon (11½-liter) crock and stir well. Place the meat in the crock and weigh the meat down with an overturned plate; put a rock on top of the plate if necessary to keep the meat submerged. Put the crock in your spare refrigerator or any safe place where the temperature will be 45°F (7°C) or below—but not below freezing—for 10 days.

2. At the end of 10 days, remove the meat and rinse. Now, you can either cook the meat immediately, or freeze it for future use.

Cooking

1. Place the meat in a Dutch oven and cover with water. Bring to a rolling boil; the water will become frothy. Boil for a few minutes longer, then drain (this will get rid of excess salts and the foam) and add new hot water to the pot until meat is covered. Add the onions, garlic, cloves, and bay leaves. Cover and simmer for 2 hours or until fork tender.

2. Remove the meat and keep warm. Add the whole potatoes and carrots and bring the liquid to a boil; turn down to a simmer and cook the vegetables for 15 minutes. Return the meat to the liquid and add the cabbage. Cook until the cabbage is tender, about 10–15 minutes.

3. Serve the meat sliced, with horseradish or hot mustard, on a platter piled with potatoes, carrots, and cabbage.

Corned Venison: The Dry Method

Yield: 2–4 servings per 1 pound (½ kg) venison

Here's a method for people who don't own a huge crock, a spare refrigerator, or a cool basement to simmer the corning meat for a couple of weeks. This method of corning works in a large bowl in the refrigerator—tough meat or tender, sweet or slightly rank. Use a piece of brisket if your animal was large enough to produce one of 2-inch (5-cm) thickness; otherwise bone out the shoulder blade.

Start corning the last day of February and you'll be ready for St. Patty's Day.

Corning Ingredients

1 cup (250 ml) brown sugar
2 cups (500 ml) Kosher salt or ice cream–maker salt
2 teaspoons onion powder
1 teaspoon peppercorns
½ teaspoon powdered cloves
½ teaspoon powdered allspice
¼ teaspoon powdered ginger
¼ teaspoon powdered mace
2 bay leaves, crumbled
12 whole juniper berries, dried
4 pounds (2 kg) boned and trimmed meat

Cooking Ingredients

1 bay leaf
1 pound (½ kg) carrots, in 5–6-inch (12–15-cm) lengths
8 medium potatoes
1 head cabbage, quartered

Preparation

1. Combine all the corning ingredients except meat in a large mixing bowl and stir thoroughly. Place the meat on top of the mixture and press it into the spices. Turn the meat over two or three times to rub the spices in well, making sure they cover all surfaces. Cover with a downturned plate and keep in the refrigerator 14–17 days, taking the meat out to reverse the order every 4–5 days.

2. After two weeks you can either freeze your corned venison for later use or cook it immediately.

Cooking

1. Tie the meat into a neat shape if necessary; a 4-pound (2-kg) piece of brisket and a boned shoulder would both need to be tied. Place it in a large saucepan, with water sufficient to completely cover the meat. Unlike most corned venison, do not freshen the water after 45 minutes.

2. Bring the pot to a boil, and skim off the foam as it develops. Reduce the heat and cook covered for 2 hours. Pour off the water and add clean water to cover. Bring to a boil again, and then turn it back to a simmer. Add the bay leaf and cook at least 30 minutes, until tender. A tender shoulder will take a total of 2½ hours; brisket will take longer.

2. When the corned meat is fork tender, add the carrots and potatoes. Cook for 20 minutes more, then lay the cabbage sections across the top of the meat and carrots (don't let the cabbage float around in the water) and cook another 15 minutes. Serve with mustard and green beer.

Corned Venison: The Dry Method (Photo by Eileen Clarke)

The Nature of Game

There was a bit of a rodeo outside my window this morning. It had been bitterly cold for several nights, and the deer had been sleeping in late. John and I were sitting in the living room drinking our first cup of coffee. Suddenly, a mule deer doe leapt out of the coulee and ran across the sage brush cliff not far from our front door. Not stotting; not trotting or galloping or prancing. A full out, panicky run. Right behind her, a mountain lion topped the coulee and stopped. As the lion debated the issue of breakfast or exposure to the two-lane highway just below, the rest of our resident herd of mule deer—seventeen does and fawns and one small forkhorn buck—snuck out the top of the coulee behind him.

We lined up the spotting scope, which is a permanent part of the living room decor, and tried to get a better look at the lion. He was gone. The mule deer continued to the top of the bench and stood, jumpy as any river-bottom whitetail and watching their backtrack. They could see into a section of brush coulee we couldn't see from across the road, and for a while I wondered if the lion was still trying to get downwind of them. But we never saw him again, and after twenty minutes, the deer started grazing, one always acting as sentry, until another twenty minutes passed and they wandered out across the bench.

By then, the sun was up and they might have been up and feeding anyway, eating our neighbor's winter wheat sprouts. But that's not what they had planned, and between the running and the nervous watching, they burned valuable calories. Calories they needed to keep them warm at ten below.

It made me think what would have happened if the lion had chased the Angus bulls on our side of the highway. We've had a problem with mountain lions the last couple of years, and the highway isn't much of a barrier. There's no fence on one side and only four-strand barbed wire on the other. Traffic is limited to a dozen families up the canyon going to work or school, logging trucks, and local ranchers taking their cattle to market once or twice a year.

This is cattle country, after all. If that lion had crossed the road, he would have been peppered with buckshot, or at least run off with a pickup truck before he took his first bite of a $25,000 Angus bull.

The occasional rodeo is a regular part of a game animal's life—as are crusted snow, drought, over-population, and subdivisions plopped down right in the middle of winter range. And before early humans domesticated the wild aurochs, that Angus bull was out there too, buffeted by the arbitrary whims of our beneficent and gentle Mother Nature and the not so whimsical nature of advancing civilization.

Mountain lions chasing deer isn't pretty. It never was pretty. But just for a moment, imagine cattle in the wilderness. Or turn the tables and imagine deer down on the farm, elk pastured on irrigated meadows, vaccinated against illness, doctored for injuries, force-fed at feedlots before slaughter, then slaughtered, butchered, and transported to market under controlled conditions. Moose fed alfalfa hay as soon as the grass loses its protein. Antelope left lazy in the fields, protected not only from mountain lions, but grizzly bears and their own hormonal excesses. What if caribou were brought to market when the meat was prime, and not when the hunter happened across it in the woods? That's the difference between domestic meat and wild game. Some wild meat is prime, better than anything the commercial American beef rancher can present at the table. Some shows the effects of nature or our mishandling.

As hunters, we do our best to bring home a healthy animal. But sometimes you can't tell, in that split second, how well you'll do. My friend Jim Atkinson once shot a raghorn elk near Gardiner, Montana, just outside of Yellowstone Park. He planned to hang it in his garage to age a few days, expecting the young bull to provide delicious meat for the winter. But as he field dressed it, he noticed the meat was green and slimy. The animal had been sick, probably with pneumonia, maybe as a result of overpopulation. The meat was inedible.

Hunting the high plains (Photo by Sil Strung)

I was luckier this year. Two weeks into our big game season, I shot a mule deer buck with enormous antlers—enormous for a meat hunter like me, anyway. The neck wasn't swollen very much yet, but I was concerned about the musk. As we started to field dress him, I leaned down and smelled the meat and was relieved. It was sweet, like any good meat should smell. Then my husband John ran his knife up the side of the sternum, and a large pocket of greenish liquid oozed out from under the hide. There was a pocket a foot long and six to eight inches high along the upper rib cage. Maybe he got into a fight with another buck. Maybe he fell. We found no other sign of injury on the animal, no clue as to what had caused this one, and once we cleaned out the injured area, the meat was as sweet and tender as any healthy buck.

Was it a drought year with no grass? Or a wet year with grass up to the deer's withers? It's all out of our control, and feed has an immense effect on flavor. It was wet in Montana in 1993; every animal I saw was fat and healthy. It was dry in 1994; the three deer I helped butcher had no fat reserves at all. The Angus cattle did. Our neighbor fed supplemental hay all summer. The elk moved into town and started eating iris; antelope will wipe out all the gardens and ornamental flowers on the Montana Hi-Line in a dry year. One year along the Musselshell River, the whitetails became so overpopulated—from a combination of open winters and lots of grain fields—they started dying off from Blue Tongue Disease. The Angus herd would have been thinned out, or doctored to prevent catastrophic loss.

Some say that you should never shoot a big bull or buck in rut, as the hormones make the meat bad. Truth is, some of the best eating I've ever had was a 4x4 whitetail, neck swollen, prowling the woods looking for a place to sack out for a couple of hours in the middle of the rut. I've never had a bad antelope—rutting buck or fat, grazing doe. On the other hand, my cousin Eric had a bad, young, mule deer doe. She had apparently run herself ragged during the rut, which puts to rest the theory that the male of the species is the only one out prowling the woods.

Then there's the young cow elk John took several years ago. She was so fat, had been eating so much good, high-protein feed that I found she tasted a little like liver, a taste that I don't particularly relish, and I spent a lot of time seasoning the meat in an effort to hide the taste.

All those things you can't control, from weather to hormones, to deer falling down in the woods—whether you hear it or not—effect the taste and texture of the meat. Ranchers can manipulate genes and feed, predators, market factors, and even rain. Hunters have to operate within strict confines.

An old rancher from eastern Washington once told me he didn't hunt anymore because it had become too stylized. Well, I'm still young, and hunting is an important part of my life. The only way I've ever hunted is by seasons and boundaries, and time-outs—stalks called on account of darkness and antis who all seem to live in cities of over 100,000 people and have no idea what subsistence hunting is, or how much rain twelve inches a year isn't. I'm not going to stop hunting because there are some rules—especially when most of them make perfect sense. Most people play by the rules and do their best to draw down on healthy animals, but once in a while, even if you do everything right, you bring home an animal that's not Grade A #1 Prime.

I believe at least half of what people call gamy, however, is fear of the unknown. When I was eighteen years old, I ran away to California to find my fortune. My first job was as a mother's helper for $50 a month. I lived in the family's basement. Supper the first night was an indefinable blob of gray meat—allegedly a forkhorn mule deer—boiled all day in water and coffee grounds to get the gamy taste out. That same woman always served white bread because she didn't like crunchy things in her bread. Perhaps it's older than history. Cave people eating in less than sanitary conditions wanting to know what it was their child was chewing on. In the twentieth century people expect life to be safe,

predictable, and sterile. You take a piece of beef, pork, lamb, or chicken and cook it; it's been inspected, certified, categorized, graded and stamped, cellophaned, and guaranteed double your money back it will taste exactly like the last piece of meat you bought. Well, thank God game meat is none of that.

Hunters take an enormous leap of faith when they take the shot. Each species has a characteristic flavor: from elk to whitetail, from musk ox to ewe sheep. But then, each individual animal is affected by its health, habitat, and everyday life. The hunter doesn't know if that animal before him or her has been harassed out of its bed every morning by mountain lions; or if the five-point bull elk got beaten up by a six-point three weeks ago and is still bruised and battered. One spring evening a couple years ago, one of our neighbor's black Angus bulls walked through the fence and onto the highway. It was dark, and he totaled a 1985 Buick Riviera. Since it wasn't his first Buick Riviera, and the bull was fairly well past his prime, our neighbor decided to send him to market. But first, he let him hang around the pasture for two months letting the bruises heal, because bruises make for awful burger and that was all he was good for at his age.

A friend of mine once tried to explain the difference between living in New York City and living in Montana. He said, "Living in New York is like being kicked to death every day by jackrabbits." I sometimes think that's the difference between domestically raised animals and those foraging in the wild. There are times when I wish I knew just which buck, doe, cow, or calf had been kicked daily by jackrabbits, hit by Buick Rivieras, or rousted from its bed and chased by mountain lions. But I will always prefer the not knowing to eating supposedly safe, commercially raised meat. I'm a hunter, not a rancher. That spotting scope in my living room will never get pointed at the Angus on my side of the highway. I prefer to be startled by something I wasn't expecting to see. And I prefer to eat game.

BIRDS AND SMALL GAME

Birds of a Feather

To my mind, there is no group of game animals more different from each other than birds. You can divide them by classes: herbivores and carnivores (except we don't eat the carnivores); or migratory and non-migratory; upland birds and waterfowl. Among waterfowl, there are surface feeders and bottom feeders. In upland circles, there are birds that fly just a little way off and set down again when flushed, and birds that get up and fly to Denver. Birds that live next to a mountain stream eat aspen buds; birds that live in the Great American Desert scratch out a living one year out of five on Starve To Death Creek. Or Froze to Death Creek. It all affects the taste and tenderness and the way

End of a day bird hunting (Photo by Eileen Clarke)

Chukars tend to the opposite. While they live in open country, it's hilly, so they don't have to fly far to be out of sight. They do however, run, and consequently have tough legs. Pheasants are the most variable. While preserve birds are all young and tender all over, wild roosters are notorious for tough legs at any age. Old roosters can be tough all over, and still have pale meat.

Hungarian partridges and doves both live in open farm land and fly a lot from field to field, and migrate in the winter as well. Thus, they tend to have darker meat. Mourning doves have dark breasts, but right along the breast bone there's a thin strip of light meat. The legs are tiny, dark, and tough to boot. The legs of any bird that lives in

you have to cook them. Arbitrarily, let's create a food chain, starting with the most pale and tender, ending with the dark and tough, and begin by saying there are exceptions to everything.

There's a reason ruffed and blue grouse are revered in old birder circles. Their lives consist of flying from the forest floor to the limbs a few feet above to nibble on aspen buds. They're built for short bursts of flight, as any bird hunter knows, and their meat is pale, tender, and mild because of that. Their kin, the spruce or Franklin grouse, is equally delicious, but do not have the reputation among hard-cores because instead of being built for bursts, they're programmed to cower. They're also programmed to change their diet—as are the blue grouses. While ruffed continue to eat aspen buds and leaves over the winter, spruce and blues can switch to conifers in the late fall, making their meat bitter. Still tender, just not sweet.

Quail and chukars are both made up of mostly light meat. Quail live in open farm country, and since they have to fly a distance to escape predators and find food, they tend to have a slightly darker breast than leg.

open spaces—from doves and Huns to chukars, quail, sage grouse, and sharptails—are tough. They just walk around more than mountain grouse, and the more you use a muscle, the more the muscle develops a good, heavy blood supply to keep it oxygenated. Thus dark meat. Flush a covey of grouse, and if you had x-ray vision, you could see them set down twenty feet (6 m) away. Sage grouse? You'd need telescopic x-ray vision to see where they land. In open country, that's the survival technique for wild creatures. (Antelope do the same, but they generally give you one last look over their shoulder—in range, if you were born lucky—before they all go into overdrive.)

Of all the upland birds I know, the most problematic for taste are sage and sharptail grouse. It's hard to remember they're related to the blue and ruffed when they're rolling around on your tongue, releasing what can only technically be called the flavor of sage. This isn't that mild, slightly sweet sage in the Spice Islands jar. It's *wild* sage, and wild sage's natural sap, creosote. All the other upland birds listed above can be put in a game bag, or hung from your shoulder and walked

Previous page: *Bird dog and mallard (Photo by Sil Strung)*

around until you reach your limit, then thrown on ice and taken back to the motel to dress. Do that with a prairie grouse, and they won't be good for much of anything except taxidermy.

Care for sage and sharptail grouse, and for any bird you suspect will be stronger tasting than you'd like, begins by drawing the digestive tract as soon as you pick it up. If you have water, wash it out as well. Then put it on ice, ASAP. The heart can be quite good in prairie grouse, so if you're into organ meat, save the heart and put it on ice, too. It can be parboiled, or just sliced and fried, or chopped into giblets for gravy.

If you can't gut the bird immediately or wash it out, toss salt inside the body cavity once you do draw it. The salt will draw the blood and bitter taste out, instead of letting it migrate into the breast meat. Leave the salt in while the bird ages, then rinse it before freezing. If it's a strong-tasting bird—you'll smell it in the blood and especially the intestines as you work with it—soak it overnight before cooking, either in a brine solution or milk. That will draw more of the bitter flavors out of the meat. And while you can cook the breasts any way you want, save the sage grouse legs for enchiladas.

I can hear someone in the back of the room saying, "What's wrong with legs?" Well, there's nothing wrong with legs. But once again, wild birds are no more like commercially raised chickens than venison is like a fatted calf. They're not pampered and fed, housed and doctored. The legs are different from the breasts on most wild birds, and they need to be cooked differently. In our freezer, we have a large, resealable freezer bag dedicated to legs. The breasts, we double wrap in good freezer paper and stuff them in the depths of the freezer. The leg bag stays on top, so we can add legs all season long: pheasants, chukars, and sharptail grouse—whatever birds we think will have tough legs. Every now and then, we take a bunch of them out, boil them up, and make delicious, spicy, multi-species enchiladas. We've tried it the other way, but by the time the legs are tender, the breasts chew like canvas. Keep a leg bag. Put a vintage pin-up photo of Betty Grable on it—or Arnold Schwarzenegger doing leg lifts.

Darker, but not always as strong tasting as sage grouse can get, are waterfowl. While I've never had a goose I didn't like, ducks vary according to what and how they eat. Surface feeders, generally, are milder tasting, these include mallards, teal, pintails, and puddle ducks such as gadwalls and widgeons. The bottom feeders are muddier tasting; these include redheads, spoonbills or shovelers, ring necks, and goldeneyes. But watch out for exceptions. Canvasback used to have a reputation for great taste. Traditionally, they lived and fed on the wild celery in Chesapeake Bay. But several years ago, my husband John had a canvasback and it was terrible. He discovered that the wild celery had fallen prey to pollution, and the canvasbacks were now feeding on everything every other bottom feeder was eating. It tasted muddy. You almost need a scorecard sometimes, or a flight schedule: mallards that have just migrated from the grain fields of Alberta taste much milder than mallards that have sat on a lake for two months. Watercress that's alive and green makes a better-tasting bird than watercress that's frozen and rotting.

Then there are migratory bog birds: snipe, rails, and woodcocks (they're hunted upland, but they live and eat bog) all have strong, slightly liver-tasting meat. Some people prefer to have a bird with distinctive flavors. They probably would like an unreconstructed stud sage grouse as well.

Almost as diverse as birds are those who hunt them, from their methods to their shotguns, their clothing, and even the state in which they bring the bag to the kitchen—never mind how their methods of aging and cooking birds differ as well. European big-game hunters claim a long tradition of bells and bugles, but I would argue that bird hunting—even in the heathen and unwashed New World—carries more myths, legends, and traditions than any other form of sport: from the hunters who won't shoot a bird with anything less than a Parker, a pointer, and a six-hundred-year-old wagon, to the hunter who won't sit a waterfowl blind without a waxed coat and hand-carved decoys. Some won't shoot birds on the ground—unless they're turkeys. And some, like the fifth-generation Montana rancher, won't shoot anything but a .22 for birds, and they mean exclusively pheasant and mountain grouse when they talk birds. If you're looking for permission to hunt Hungarian partridge, ask for them by name; ranchers usually won't care how many of those you shoot, as long as you leave their "birds" alone.

Then there are people like me who drag out a custom-stocked, English walnut Beretta Silver Snipe, and make men cringe by describing in detail the last cottontail hunt I took it on. But even I dread telling strangers I skin all my upland birds.

Plucking and Skinning

And what's the big deal about skinning a bird, anyway? Well, it's just not done in some circles. Some people pluck every feather of every bird by hand. Some hire the work out: Hutterites in central Alberta will do a duck for $2.50. And some people invest in motorized whirligigs to do the job. I know I just offended somebody with those words, but here's some more. Two more in fact: herbicides and pesticides.

All farmers use chemicals (and if they say they don't, their fathers did, or the former owner, or worse—their neighbor still does) and birds don't know fences. In short, if I'm upland hunting in neat little rows of grain—on my side of the fence or the neighbor's—and there's no sign of weeds or volunteer crops, I skin. On the other hand, I rarely skin a duck or goose. There's more fat in waterfowl skin and both fat and skin add flavor to the bird—flavors that we want to bring to the table.

Most Easterners think of the West as a pristine wilderness. Not quite true. There's hardly an inch in Montana, for instance, that some homesteader didn't try to cut a plow into—including the top of Square Butte—and if that wasn't enough, Montana is home to the #1 Superfund site in the United States. For about fifty years a copper company dumped mining waste onto the ground, which leached into streams and ground water with every rain, and is now backed up behind a dam that the EPA is afraid to touch for fear it will release the pollutants downstream into as yet relatively clean waters. I wouldn't hunt waterfowl there. I wouldn't put my waders in that water much less put anything that lives and eats in and on that water in my mouth. You choose your spots. Where I hunt waterfowl, I don't worry about skinning. When I hunt a new place, I read up about it, so I feel safe eating plucked birds.

Whether you're plucking upland birds or waterfowl, there are two good times for dry plucking. The best time is immediately after the shot, within the first fifteen minutes and up to thirty minutes. Once *rigor mortis* sets in, the feathers set up and are hard to pluck. So wait a few days and pluck it when it's done aging and

you're ready to cook or freeze the bird. It will not pluck as easily after aging as it would have in the first fifteen minutes, but sometimes you don't have a choice.

For waterfowl, there's also the wet method. It's a mess, but if you have lots of birds, and no nearby Hutterite colony willing to do the work, it's faster.

1. Half fill a 5-gallon (20-liter) bucket with water. Heat the water to 202°F (95°C) at sea level (or 10°F/5°C less than boiling). Stir in 1 teaspoon of liquid laundry detergent.

2. Immerse 2–4 ducks at a time, and stir them gently in the water for about 15 seconds. Remove them when the breast and wing feathers pluck easily. Done right, the feathers should come off with a gentle rubbing motion. The detergent allows the water to penetrate the oily feathers; the water loosens the feather butts. But you must keep the temperature constant and not under- or over-process the birds. If you leave the birds in too long, the feathers will set even harder.

Then there's the hot-wax method: Melt about $700 of paraffin in a pot and dip the birds; let cool. You'll be able to peel the feathers off in sheets. This is the fastest, easiest way and, of course, costs the most.

Aging

When it comes to aging, there are at least four choices. Your first option is to not age the bird at all; second, to age it one to seven days outdoors; third to hang it from the neck until the body is so tender it falls off the head; and fourth, to draw and wash the bird and place it in a plastic bag in the bottom of your no-frost refrigerator for one to seven days. (Older-model refrigerators—the ones that build-up ice—won't dry out the bird as much, so you can use a paper bag.) Since all birds can benefit from a little aging, let's eliminate method number one. Number two can be pretty iffy, depending on the weather. Number three is the traditional Old World method, and one that Norm and Sil have used successfully for years; this method includes leaving the innards in. Norm always said, "If you're going to eat wild birds, they shouldn't taste like commercial chicken." If you like strong flavors this is a tried-and-true method of aging. Personally, I don't like strong game flavors, so I prefer option number four.

A lot of people will tell you they don't age their birds at all and they chew just fine. I suggest that 80–90 percent of all birds shot are the young of the year. By the time you finish your day's hunt, get them home, and freeze them, they've been aging anywhere from eight to thirty-six hours. They're young birds and that's all they need. The occasional tough bird people complain about was probably a wily older bird that should have been aged longer. To tell if a bird is less than a year old, try to bend the beak. If it gives, it's this year's hatch; if it's hard, it's older. Rooster pheasants have two other criteria to age them: their spurs and tail feathers. A tail feather of twenty-two inches (55 cm) is indicative of a wily old rooster, as is a hard, sharp spur. All birds we suspect of being older than this year's hatch we age in the bottom of the refrigerator for 4–7 days.

The first wild bird I ever ate was a rooster pheasant my ex-husband shot in 1967. He'd never killed one before and decided since his favorite method of eating chicken was roasted, he'd roast this pheasant. So he skinned it and stuck it in an open roasting pan, and roasted the stuffing out of it, since he was afraid that a wild bird might carry disease. I was amazed, because it was the first thing I ever saw him cook. Then he brought it to the table. It was tough and dry, and ugly to boot. I don't think we ate more than two or three bites. While there are many things I've forgiven my ex for in the last twenty-three years, that one sticks with me.

Shoot them with Parkers, Berettas, AYAs, or the shotgun your grandfather bought at Sears. Wear jeans, brushed twill, brush pants, or Carhardt. Ground sluice, wing shoot, pass shoot, or decoy. Pluck, skin, or dip them in a vat of hot wax. But when you cook them, you better know what you're doing. No wild bird deserves to be cooked into shoe leather.

Sharptail grouse (Photo by Sil Strung)

MOUNTAIN GROUSE OVER RISOTTO

Yield: 4 servings

Risotto is not a walk-away dish. Like the directions on a shampoo bottle, you lather-rinse-repeat, lather-rinse-repeat—and keep stirring the whole time. The good news is it only takes about 25–30 minutes, which is also how long the birds take to cook.

Ruffed grouse male drumming (Photo by Erwin and Peggy Bauer)

The first time I met Steve Bodio, author of *Rage for Falcons*, he made me this dish, insisted I pronounce risotto without the final "o," and swore the recipe was a family secret. With his permission, here is Mountain Grouse over Risott'.

Roasting Ingredients

2 blue or ruffed grouse, plucked; chukar is
   equally good
Olive oil, a splash to wipe the birds
Salt and pepper, to taste
2 lemon slices

Risotto Ingredients

2 quarts (2 liters) stock
3 tablespoons butter
2 teaspoons olive oil
1 scallion, finely chopped
2 cups (500 ml) arborio rice or medium grain
   white rice

Salt and pepper, to taste
½ cup (125 ml) dry red wine
½ cup (125 ml) Parmesan cheese, freshly
   grated

Cooking the Grouse

1. Preheat the oven to 350°F (175°C), and start the birds just before you start the risotto. Rub the outside of the bird with olive oil and salt, and insert a slice of lemon in the body cavity. Place on a rack in a roasting pan and set in the center of the oven. Now do steps 1–3 for cooking the risotto.

2. Cooking time varies with the weight of the bird but will be no more than 30 minutes or they'll dry out. Set a timer for 25 minutes and then keep checking. Pierce the breast; the juice will run clear when the bird is done, just like chicken. Take the birds out, cover with foil. Then do step 4 of the risotto.

Cooking the Risotto

1. Set the stock at a low boil, and keep it hot while you're fixing the rice.

2. In a large cast-iron skillet, heat 2 tablespoons of the butter and all the olive oil at medium heat, until the foaming subsides. Sauté the scallion. Pour in all the rice along with the salt and pepper. Turn and mix the rice until each grain is coated; continue mixing until the rice looks chalky. Constantly stir or the rice will stick and burn.

3. Pour in the wine—it will hiss and steam— and mix thoroughly. Immediately follow with about ½ cup (125 ml) of the hot stock. Stir the rice so that all the liquid gets thoroughly mixed in, and keep stirring often so nothing sticks. Keep uncovered on medium heat, and cook until a swipe through the pan with whatever you are using to stir shows the bottom of the pan is almost dry. Then add ⅓ cup (80 ml) more broth. When a swipe through the pan again shows the bottom to be almost dry, add ⅓ cup (80 ml) of broth. Repeat. Repeat. Repeat. Repeat. The pan should get dry every 3–4 minutes or less.

4. After 15 minutes you should be tasting the rice before you add broth each time. After about 20 minutes, the rice will start getting creamy. When the grains start to get chewy rather than hard, start adding less broth each time, but keep repeating the process until the rice grains are about like *al dente* pasta. Add 2–3 tablespoons more stock, stir until it's almost dry, and turn off the heat.

5. Your timer should be ringing: check the grouse. Take them out of the oven and set them aside. Now go back to the risotto. Pour in all the Parmesan and 1 tablespoon butter. Mix thoroughly.

6. Immediately serve the grouse and risotto, topped with freshly ground black pepper and more Parmesan.

LEMON PHEASANT

Yield: 4–6 servings

This recipe is a wonderful sweet-tart way to cook pheasant. Lemon zest adds a tangy flavor. Zest is the yellow part of the lemon rind. A zester removes it without taking the bitter white underneath, but you can use a grater as well. To make retrieval of the zest easier, line the grader with plastic wrap first, grate, then remove the plastic and just wipe off the zest.

Top: *Pheasant hunting (Photo by Eileen Clarke)*

Bottom: *Lemon Pheasant (Photo by Eileen Clarke)*

Ingredients

2 pheasants
2 cups (500 ml) lemon juice
1 cup (250 ml) flour
1 tablespoon paprika
1 teaspoon white pepper
½ cup (125 ml) canola oil or extra-virgin olive oil
¼ cup (60 ml) brown sugar
1 teaspoon lemon extract
½ cup (125 ml) chicken bouillon
2 tablespoons lemon zest
2 lemons, sliced thin

Preparation

1. Quarter the pheasants and place them in a deep bowl with 2 cups (500 ml) lemon juice. Cover and refrigerate at least 12–24 hours, turning occasionally.

Cooking

1. Drain and dry the pheasant quarters and set aside. Place flour, 1 teaspoon of paprika, and all the pepper in a large plastic bag. Then place pheasant in the bag, 2–3 pieces at a time, and shake to coat.
2. Lightly fry the birds in hot oil in a Dutch oven, a few pieces at a time. As each piece achieves a light gold color, place it in a single layer in a large shallow baking dish; a 9x13-inch (22x32-cm) pan is a squeeze; a little bigger is better.
3. Preheat oven to 350°F (175°C). Mix the brown sugar and lemon extract in the chicken stock and pour over the top. Now sprinkle with the lemon zest, layer the sliced lemons over the top, and sprinkle the last of the paprika over all.
4. Bake uncovered for 40 minutes.

MOUNTAIN GROUSE WITH COUSCOUS STUFFING

Yield: 6–8 servings

Mountain grouse, chukars, or pheasant—you can use all the same bird, or a medley of birds with light meat. It all tastes wonderful, and it's all made in a clay cooker to keep the birds moist. If you don't have a clay cooker, use a covered roasting pan and lay a piece of cheese-cloth moistened in butter, margarine, or olive oil over each bird.

Couscous Ingredients
½ cup (125 ml) lemon juice
½ cup (125 ml) water
1 tablespoon butter
⅔ cup (160 ml) instant couscous
1 clove garlic, minced
2 green onions, diced
¼ cup (60 ml) diced cilantro
Dash of cayenne
Dash of paprika
½ teaspoon cumin
½ cup (125 ml) chicken bouillon

Roasting Ingredients
4 mountain grouse, whole (or any small
    birds with light meat)
6 carrots, cut into 1-inch (2½-cm) lengths

Cooking
1. Make the couscous by heating the lemon juice, water, and butter to boiling. Add the couscous and turn off the heat. Cover and let steep 5 minutes.
2. Into the couscous, stir the garlic, onion, cilantro, cayenne, paprika, cumin, and enough bouillon to moisten.
3. Prepare the clay pot by soaking 10–15 minutes in water. Do *not* preheat the oven. Once the clay pot is soaked, set the birds inside, one at a time, and stuff them with the couscous mixture, strewing the excess couscous mixture over the birds. Cut the carrots over the top.
4. Cover and place in a *cold* oven. Turn the oven to 450°F (230°C) and cook for 50 minutes. If you want to brown the birds, take the top off after 50 minutes and cook uncovered 5–10 minutes more.

Chukar (Photo by Erwin and Peggy Bauer)

PHEASANT WITH PEACHES

Yield: 2–4 servings

This is a wonderful way of preparing a bird that normally is dry. There are quite a few steps to this but the results are well worth it.

Above:
Pheasant with Peaches ready for the oven (Photo by Sil Strung)

Right:
Pheasant with Peaches (Photo by Sil Strung)

Ingredients

1 can of peach halves, 29 ounces (823 g)
2 tablespoons lemon juice
3 tablespoons white port wine or cognac
1 pheasant, quartered
2 carrots, thinly sliced lengthwise
1 onion, sliced thin
$\frac{1}{4}$ teaspoon salt
$\frac{1}{4}$ teaspoon pepper
Pinch of powdered thyme
Pinch of powdered sage
Pinch of allspice
2 tablespoons sugar
$\frac{1}{4}$ cup (60 ml) red wine vinegar
2 cups (500 ml) chicken bouillon
2 tablespoons cornstarch

Cooking

1. Drain the peaches and discard the liquid. Place the peaches in a small bowl with lemon juice and wine, and let them marinate for at least 30 minutes.

2. Preheat oven to 425°F (220°C). Place the pheasant in a small roasting pan with the carrots, onion, salt, pepper, thyme, sage, and allspice. Roast uncovered for 15 minutes. Turn the oven down to 300°F (150°C) and continue to roast until done, about 30 minutes, turning the pheasant quarters once or twice.

3. While the pheasant is cooking, bring the sugar and vinegar to a boil in a medium-sized saucepan, stirring constantly. Keep it boiling for several minutes or until browned and caramelized, watching carefully so it doesn't burn.

Remove from the heat, and slowly add half the bouillon. Return the pan to the burner and gently simmer to dissolve the caramelized mixture. Combine the cornstarch with the rest of the bouillon and add to the pan. Continue to cook until thickened, about 3–4 minutes. Then add the drained peaches and heat thoroughly.

4. When the pheasant is done, remove to a serving platter. Remove peaches from the sauce with a slotted spoon and place them around the pheasant on the same platter. To the roaster, add the peach sauce and blend thoroughly with the pan juices. Pour some of this sauce over the pheasant. Save the rest in a small pitcher. Serve with rice and asparagus.

QUAIL IN CABBAGE LEAVES

Yield: 2–4 servings

I originally tasted this meal in Mexico. Norm and I were invited to a ranch that had literally hundreds of quail. Sometimes I'd even shoot three birds with one shot, which was good because it takes two to make a meal for each person.

Quail in Cabbage Leaves (Photo by Sil Strung)

Ingredients

1 head of cabbage
4 whole quail, with heart and liver
2 eggs, hard-boiled, then chopped
1 green onion, minced
1 teaspoon dried parsley
Salt and pepper, to taste
1 cup (250 ml) brandy

Cooking

1. Carefully remove the large outer leaves of the cabbage. Bring a large pot of water to a rolling boil. Lower heat to a simmer and gently place the leaves into the water and cook until they become limp. Remove with a slotted spoon and set aside.

2. In a small saucepan, parboil the heart and liver. Remove and chop, then stir together with the egg, onion, parsley, salt, and pepper. Preheat oven to 300°F (150°C). Divide the stuffing evenly, and stuff the birds. Wrap each bird in a cabbage leaf and secure with thread before placing in a casserole dish. Pour the brandy around the sides.

3. Bake covered for 2 hours and serve.

SOUTHWEST PARTRIDGE

Ingredients for Southwest Partridge (Photo by Eileen Clarke)

Yield: 4–6 servings

Here's a quick-cooking recipe for a medium-dark bird. The squash and red peppers make this a bright and colorful dish for a cold winter's night.

Ingredients

2 tablespoons oil
2 Hungarian partridges, quartered
4 carrots, diced
1 onion, diced
5 cloves garlic, minced
1 cup (250 ml) chicken stock
$\frac{1}{2}$ cup (125 ml) orange juice
$\frac{1}{2}$ cup (125 ml) tomatoes, diced
1 tablespoon dried rosemary
2 tablespoons sherry
Salt and pepper, to taste
$\frac{1}{2}$ yellow summer squash, sliced $\frac{1}{4}$ inch ($\frac{1}{2}$ cm) thick
$\frac{1}{2}$ small zucchini, sliced $\frac{1}{4}$ inch ($\frac{1}{2}$ cm) thick
1 red sweet pepper, sliced $\frac{1}{4}$ inch ($\frac{1}{2}$ cm) thick

Cooking

1. In 1 tablespoon of oil in a Dutch oven, lightly brown the Hungarian partridges on a medium setting and set aside. Add 1 more tablespoon of oil, and brown the carrots, onions, and garlic.

2. Return the Huns to the pot; add stock, orange juice, tomatoes, rosemary, sherry, salt, and pepper. Bring the mixture to a gentle boil and simmer covered for 40 minutes.

3. Add squash, zucchini, and red pepper, and simmer uncovered 5–10 minutes longer, until zucchini just starts to fold. Serve over rice.

Southwest Partridge (Photo by Eileen Clarke)

PHEASANT CHOWDER

Yield: 6–8 servings

This recipes combines rice and pheasant in a cream-based soup that has a surprise ingredient and flavor. You can also make it low-fat without the cream, and it's still delicious.

Pheasant Chowder (Photo by Eileen Clarke)

Ingredients

2 large or 3 small pheasants or a dozen legs
2 large onions, quartered
2 celery stalks, diced
1 cup (250 ml) rice, raw
2 cucumbers, peeled and puréed
¼ cup (60 ml) white wine
2 teaspoons dill weed, or more to taste
Salt and pepper, to taste
2 cups (500 ml) half and half or non-fat yogurt

Cooking

1. Put the pheasant, frozen or thawed, into a soup pot with the onions, celery, and enough water to cover—about 8 cups (2 liters). Boil gently until the meat easily pulls from the bones, about 90 minutes.

2. Remove the pheasants to cool, and save the broth. Remove the meat from the bones and cut into bite-sized chunks and set aside. Discard the onions and celery. (You can do all this ahead of time and freeze the broth in ice-cube trays.)

3. Add the rice to the broth and bring to a boil. Turn down the heat to a simmer and cook, covered, until the rice is tender. Add the puréed cucumbers, pheasant meat, wine, dill, salt, and pepper to the broth. Bring the pot almost to a boil, then remove from the heat and add the half-and-half. Serve.

PHEASANT POT ROAST

Yield: 4 servings

A perfect dish for a tough, older bird—and a delightfully tangy sauce to boot.

Ringneck pheasants (Photo by Sil Strung)

Ingredients

1 mature pheasant
1 tablespoon olive oil
1 tablespoon butter
⅔ cup (160 ml) stock or broth
2 onions, sliced
½ pound (250 g) carrots, sliced
1 rutabaga, cubed
4 potatoes, quartered
2 medium bay leaves
1 teaspoon powdered thyme
2 slices bacon
4–6 tablespoons flour
½ cup (125 ml) hearty dry red wine

Cooking

1. In a Dutch oven, brown the pheasant on all sides in the olive oil and butter. Add the broth, vegetables, and spices, and cover the bird with the bacon. Bring the broth to a boil, and reduce the heat. Simmer, covered, for about 45 minutes.
2. Remove the bird and vegetables and set aside on a warm platter. Add 4–6 tablespoons flour to the red wine, stir until smooth, and then add to the juices and stir up the tasty bits from the bottom. Simmer the juices and stir continuously until the sauce thickens.
3. Serve the pheasant quartered—with a bit of bacon over each piece—with the vegetables and the sauce over all.

PHEASANT À LA KING

Yield: 2–4 servings

We use pheasant here, but any bird with light meat, like chukar and grouse—even cottontail rabbit—will work just as well.

Ingredients

¼ cup (60 ml) butter
3 tablespoons flour
1 cup (250 ml) chicken broth
½ cup (125 ml) whipping cream
Salt and pepper, to taste
2 cups (500 ml) cooked and diced pheasant
½ teaspoon sherry
4 croissants or toasted bread with crusts
    removed
Parsley, to garnish

Cooking

1. In a medium-size sauce pan, melt the butter and stir in the flour. Cook for 1–2 minutes, add chicken broth and cream, and stir until smooth. Season with salt and pepper to taste.

2. Place the pheasant in the sauce and heat thoroughly, but do not boil as the cream will curdle. Stir in the sherry, and serve on toasted croissants. Sprinkle with parsley.

Pheasant hunting
(Photo by
Eileen Clarke)

Comparison of wild birds, from left: quail, two Hungarian partridges, sharptail grouse, and pheasant (Photo by Eileen Clarke)

Dove or Quail en Brochette

Yield: 4 servings

I went to a shooting preserve in Mexico and wound up eating a duck, a quail, and a dove all by myself. I normally have a small appetite, but when birds are prepared *en brochette*, even the lightest eater will need at least two.

For grilling it will help if you skewer the legs together with toothpicks to keep them from dangling in the coals.

Basting Ingredients

¼ cup (60 ml) margarine
½ teaspoon paprika
¼ teaspoon salt
¼ teaspoon pepper
⅛ teaspoon powdered cloves
⅛ teaspoon cayenne
⅛ teaspoon nutmeg
⅛ teaspoon celery salt

Brochette Ingredients

½ pound (250 g) bacon, cut in 2-inch (5-cm) lengths
8 doves or quails
2 whole tomatoes, quartered
1 onion, quartered
1 zucchini, cut into chunks
1 can pineapple chunks, 8 ounces (227 g), drained

Preparation

1. Melt the margarine. Combine the spices, add them to the margarine, and mix thoroughly. Preheat the gas grill to high for 10 minutes, then turn down to medium, or start 4–5 dozen briquettes.

2. Fold each piece of bacon in half. Skewer the birds, vegetables, and pineapple on kabob skewers starting and alternating everything with the folded bacon. Make certain the birds are surrounded by bacon.

3. Baste the birds with the margarine mixture.

Cooking

1. Grill slowly, and baste at least twice, until the vegetables are done. The birds will also be done, but test by pricking the breast with a fork; the juices will run clear when done after about 15–20 minutes.

LIME DOVES

Yield: 2–4 servings

Easy summer or winter, grilled or hot fried indoors, lime doves marinate in 30 minutes and cook up in seconds.

Lime Doves (Photo by Eileen Clarke)

Ingredients
Breasts of 6 doves
½ cup (125 ml) lime juice
4–6 drops Tabasco Jalapeño Sauce
1 tablespoon butter

Preparation
1. Fillet the dove breasts from the back down, leaving both sides connected at the breastbone. You should end up with a butterfly of meat about the size of your palm and about ¼ inch (½ cm) thick.

2. In a bowl, pour the lime juice over the meat, add the Tabasco Jalapeño Sauce, and let marinate for 30 minutes only. If you marinate longer, the meat will have a bitter taste.

Cooking
1. Heat up a frying pan. Coat it with butter just before you place each fillet on it, then cook about 1 minute to a side. (Alternatively, you can barbecue over hot coals.) Serve with grilled onions and rice, or potato salad and cole slaw.

HUNGARIAN PARTRIDGES IN FRIED RICE

Yield: 2 servings

I thought Norm and I always kept a well-stocked camper, but we proved it one day in central Montana. We were on a week-long bird-hunting expedition, and hit the Hungarian partridge jackpot. Huns in Fried Rice was invented on the spot: the kicker was we even had the almonds on board.

Ingredients

2 Hungarian partridges, split in half
2 cups (500 ml) chicken stock or broth
Salt and pepper, to taste
2 tablespoons butter
3 green onions, chopped
2 cloves garlic, minced
½ cup (125 ml) crushed vermicelli noodles
1½ cups (375 ml) instant rice
3 tablespoons parsley
½ teaspoon celery salt
2 tablespoons slivered almonds, toasted or sautéed

Cooking

1. Boil the Huns gently in chicken broth, with salt and pepper to taste, until tender, about 15 minutes. With a slotted spoon, remove the birds from the broth and set aside to cool. Reserve the broth. When cooled, take the meat from the bones and place the meat back in the broth.

2. In a heavy sauce pan, melt the butter over medium heat and sauté the onions and garlic for a few minutes. Add the vermicelli to the pan and brown lightly, about 1–2 minutes. When browned, add the broth to the pan. Pour in the instant rice and season with parsley and celery salt. Remove from the heat, and cover for 5 minutes or until the rice is flaky.

3. To serve, put the birds and rice on a platter and garnish with the almonds.

Hungarian partridges (Photo by Sil Strung)

B&B PARTRIDGE

Yield: 4–6 servings

The recipe does not get its name from a fancy inn. Instead, this is a recipe full of "Bs" for wild-tasting birds: beer, barley, broth, bay leaf, and a touch of brown sugar. This is an ideal recipe for Hungarian partridge, doves, and chukars that haven't been living the high life.

Hungarian partridges (Photo by John Barsness)

Ingredients

1 tablespoon cooking oil
2 Hungarian partridges, diced, or leave legs whole
1 onion, diced
6 tablespoons flour
1 can medium-dark beer, 12 ounces (360 ml)
2½ cups (625 ml) chicken stock or broth
2 cups (500 ml) diced carrots
¾ cup (185 ml) barley
1–2 tablespoons brown sugar, to taste
1 bay leaf
½ teaspoon thyme leaf
Pepper, to taste
2 cups (500 ml) frozen peas

Cooking

1. Heat 1 tablespoon oil in a Dutch oven and quickly brown the Huns. Once they are brown, push to one side, and brown the onion in the same pan.

2. Add the flour, stirring quickly to coat all the meat and onion; it will be a very dry mixture. Now add the beer, stirring again, to keep the gravy from sticking. Add the broth, then add the carrots, barley, sugar, and seasonings, and bring to a boil. Reduce heat to a simmer and cover. Cook for 45–60 minutes, until the barley is tender, stirring the bottom up three to four times to keep it from sticking.

3. Heat the peas, and add to the pot just before serving.

Note: Instead of adding barley, you can serve the stew over mashed or boiled potatoes. Reduce the chicken broth by ½ cup (125 ml) if you leave out the barley.

SHARPTAIL SOUP

Yield: 4–6 servings

A hearty soup with enough spices to stand up to this strong-flavored bird with its dark meat—without burying its distinctive taste.

Sharptail grouse (Photo by Sil Strung)

Ingredients

2 tablespoons cooking oil
2 sharptail grouse, diced into 2-inch (5-cm) chunks
2 large onions, coarsely chopped
2 cups (500 ml) celery, chopped
¼ cup (60 ml) ginger, freshly grated
1 teaspoon ground cumin
1 teaspoon ground cardamom
1 teaspoon ground coriander
½–1 teaspoon chili powder, to taste
2 cups (500 ml) chickpeas, canned or precooked and drained
2 cups (500 ml) chicken stock or bouillon

Cooking

1. In a Dutch oven, heat 1 tablespoon of the oil on medium-high setting and brown the sharptail quickly. Remove the bird from the pan and set aside. Add the second tablespoon of oil and sauté the onions and celery until tender. Add the seasonings and cook a few minutes longer, until the aroma fills the kitchen.

2. Return the browned sharptail chunks to the pan. Add the chickpeas, and stock, and salt and pepper to taste. Bring the pot to a slow boil, then turn to a simmer; cover, and cook 45–60 minutes until the sharptail is tender.

SMOTHERED SHARPTAIL

Yield: 2–4 servings

I like to use this recipe on sharptails to cover up the livery taste the older birds sometimes have.

Sauce Ingredients

2 tablespoons butter
$\frac{1}{4}$ pound (100 ml) mushrooms, sliced
2 tablespoons chopped onions
3 tablespoons flour
2 cups (500 ml) chicken stock or broth
$\frac{1}{4}$ teaspoon salt
$\frac{1}{8}$ teaspoon pepper
$\frac{1}{8}$ teaspoon nutmeg
$\frac{1}{2}$ cup (125 ml) whipping cream
$\frac{1}{2}$ teaspoon dried parsley

Sharptail Ingredients

2 tablespoons cornmeal
$\frac{1}{2}$ teaspoon dried parsley
$\frac{1}{4}$ teaspoon garlic salt
$\frac{1}{4}$ teaspoon pepper
$\frac{1}{8}$ teaspoon ground sage
$\frac{1}{8}$ teaspoon ground thyme
$\frac{1}{8}$ teaspoon ground coriander
Pinch of savory
Pinch of allspice
2 tablespoons flour
2 tablespoons butter
2 tablespoons olive oil
4 sharptail grouse breasts, sliced lengthwise
  in 1-inch ($2\frac{1}{2}$-cm) strips
1 egg, slightly beaten

Cooking the Sauce

1. In a medium-size sauce pan, melt the butter. Add the mushrooms and onions, and sauté over medium heat for 5 minutes. The mushrooms should be limp and the onions translucent.

2. Add the flour to the pan and blend. Slowly pour in the broth. Cook and stir until slightly thickened, about 5 minutes. Season with salt, pepper, and nutmeg. Keep it warm—and handy. When you're finished sautéing the breasts, you'll be adding the cream and parsley to finish the sauce, too. Now begin cooking the birds.

Cooking the Birds

1. Combine the cornmeal with the parsley, seasonings, and flour. Melt the butter in a heavy iron skillet and add the olive oil.

2. Dip the sharptail pieces first in the cornmeal mixture, then into the beaten egg, and then back into the cornmeal mixture. Sauté the breasts on medium heat, turning once, until done. They'll only take a few minutes.

3. Pour the whipping cream into the sauce, sprinkle with parsley and, as the breasts get done, place them on a serving platter. Pour some of the finished mushroom sauce over the top.

4. Pour the remaining sauce into a small pitcher for the table. If you like sherry, you can add a drop or two to the gravy.

SAGE GROUSE ENCHILADAS WITH GREEN SAUCE

Yield: 4–6 servings

This looks intimidating, but it's really pretty simple. The sauce takes about 10 minutes, the rice is instant, and who can't boil water? Take it one step at a time, and remember, while this is a mild imitation of a Mexican favorite, it can easily be adapted to be much hotter.

Sage Grouse Enchiladas with Green Sauce (Photo by Eileen Clarke)

Meat Ingredients
6 sage grouse legs
1 medium onion, quartered
1 clove garlic, whole
½ teaspoon dried leaf oregano
½ teaspoon ground cumin

Green Sauce Ingredients
2 cans diced green chilies, 4 ounces (114 g) each
½ teaspoon dried leaf oregano
¼ teaspoon garlic powder
½ teaspoon ground cumin
2 teaspoons white vinegar
1 tablespoon flour
1 cup (250 ml) water

Spice Rice Ingredients
2 cups (500 ml) cooked rice, instant
1 clove garlic
¼ teaspoon chili powder
⅛ teaspoon cumin

Assembly Ingredients
1 can refried beans, 16 ounces (454 g)
6 flour tortillas, 8 inches (20 cm) in diameter
4 tomatoes, diced
4 cups (1 liter) shredded lettuce
1 pound (½ kg) Monterey Jack or mild Cheddar cheese, coarsely grated
Nonfat yogurt (or sour cream), to taste
Tabasco Jalapeño Sauce

Cooking the Meat

1. Put all the legs in a soup pot, cover with water, and bring to a boil. Reduce heat, skim off the foam, and add the onion, garlic, and seasonings. Now cover and simmer for 2 hours.

2. Remove the legs and cool. Remove the vegetables and freeze the broth for making Mountain Grouse with Risotto or Sharptail Grouse Soup.

3. Shred the cooled meat off the legs with a fork and set aside.

Cooking the Green Sauce

1. Put all ingredients (except the flour and $\frac{1}{4}$ cup (60 ml) of the water) in a blender and purée. Pour into a small saucepan and heat to boiling. Turn down to a simmer.

2. Mix the flour and water in the blender, and add slowly to the green sauce. Continue cooking, stirring constantly, until the sauce thickens slightly. (You don't want it as thick as gravy; but not totally loosey goosey either.) Turn off the heat and set the sauce aside.

Cooking the Spice Rice

1. Cook instant rice, according to package directions, but add garlic, chili powder, and cumin to the water as you add the rice.

Assembly

1. Heat the rice, green sauce, beans, and tortillas, and arrange in bowls. I put the rice and beans in separate bowls, lay 2–3 tortillas over each and microwave until hot—between 2–3 minutes on high. Then set out the rest of the ingredients.

2. Lay one tortilla on a plate, then strew the meat of one leg and about $\frac{1}{4}$ cup each beans and rice across the center of the tortilla. Spoon about 2 tablespoons of your cooked green sauce over the filling. Roll up the tortilla.

3. Top the rolled tortilla with about 3 tablespoons of cheese. Heat the tortilla in a hot oven or microwave until the cheese melts. Spoon 3–4 tablespoons of the cooked green sauce, a dab of yogurt (or sour cream), and several dashes of Tabasco Jalapeño Sauce over the top. Garnish with lettuce and tomato.

Note: To turn up the heat, use medium or hot canned chilies for the green sauce, and red Tabasco sauce over the top.

Sage grouse male strutting (Photo by Erwin and Peggy Bauer)

WATERFOWL AND TURKEYS

DUCK BREAST PÂTÉ

Yield: 3½ cups (¾ liter)

Mallard drakes (Photo by Sil Strung)

Believe me, at the end of the party, there'll be veggie platters and wine cheese balls left on the table. This duck pâté won't make it past the first wave of grazers.

Ingredients
4 duck breast fillets
2 tablespoons olive oil
¼ cup (60 ml) onion
4 cloves garlic
12 ounces (340 g) cream cheese, softened
1 tablespoon mayonnaise
½ teaspoon sweet basil
Salt and pepper, to taste
Dash of Tabasco sauce
Fresh parsley, minced

Preparation
1. Fillet the duck breasts and sauté in olive oil until well done and crisp. Cool and purée in a food processor until they are finely chopped, almost to a powder. Remove the puréed duck breasts and set aside in a mixing bowl.

2. Into your food processor, add the onion, basil, and three of the garlic cloves. Process until minced and add to the mixing bowl. Now add 8 ounces (227 g) of the softened cream cheese and all the mayonnaise to the mixture. Beat with a mixer until well blended. Remove from the bowl and mound into two large or four small balls on wax paper on a cookie sheet. Chill well.

3. In a clean processor bowl, cream the remaining 4 ounces (114 g) of cream cheese with the remaining clove of garlic, salt, and pepper. Add Tabasco, one drop at a time, to taste. Frost the pâté balls with this mixture and then sprinkle with minced parsley. Serve at once with crackers or freeze individually for later use.

BARBECUED GINGER DUCK

Yield: 2 servings

It doesn't have to be summer to barbecue, and it doesn't have to be chicken. Ducks, geese, and wild turkey are prime candidates for the barbecue. Leave the skin on; the skin and its fat add a lot of flavor to the meat. And remember that grilling is not an exact science—not like turning the oven on to 450°. Check the birds early and often.

One important utensil that you will need for this recipe is a fully loaded water pistol to help with the barbecuing.

Ingredients

1 large duck
1½ cups (375 ml) white wine
1½ cups (375 ml) orange marmalade, low or no sugar
1 tablespoon fresh ginger, grated

Preparation

1. Rinse the duck, then fillet the breasts, and cut the legs off at the thigh joint—being careful to keep the skin on—and pat dry.
2. Mix the wine, marmalade, and ginger in a non-corrosive bowl, add the duck pieces, and let marinate 7–12 hours in the refrigerator.

Cooking

1. Start a large pile of briquettes—at least a dozen for each piece to be grilled. The larger the bird, the larger the pile, too. When they get white hot, spread them out into a dense but even pile. (If you have a propane barbecue, preheat for 10 minutes on high, and then cook the birds on high.) Remove the duck from the marinade and reserve the liquid.
2. Set the grill about 3 inches (7½ cm) above the coals and baste the meat frequently with the reserved marinade. (Use the water pistol to put out large grease fires.) Mallards will take 6–8 minutes to a side. The meat is done anywhere from rare to medium; but don't cook it to well done as the meat tends to get very livery tasting when it is overcooked.

Note: I've done this barbecue with lesser Canada geese, too. It's great, but cooking time was much longer: about 25 minutes to a side. Commercially raised birds need to be cooked until all the pink is gone, to destroy any disease.

Above:
Barbecued Ginger Duck (Photo by Eileen Clarke)

Left:
Mallard drake flushing (Photo by Erwin and Peggy Bauer)

BARBECUED DUCK

Yield: 2 servings

There are people who *say* they like duck, and then there are duck *lovers*. All I had to do was dial my friend Dick VanAusdol's number and say "Quack, quack!" He was at my door with fork in hand before I could get the barbecue fired up.

Barbecued Duck (Photo by Sil Strung)

Ingredients

1 mallard or duck, about 1¾ pounds (¾ kg)
1 teaspoon sea salt or Kosher salt
1 teaspoon garlic salt
Pinch of powdered oregano
Pinch of powdered thyme
Pinch of pepper
Pinch of allspice

Cooking

1. Split the duck down the back. Combine the salt with the garlic salt and add the oregano, thyme, pepper, and allspice, and blend. Rub these seasonings all over the bird, inside and out, with your hand.

3. Preheat the gas grill on high for 10 minutes, then turn down to medium. Place the duck in a hinged grilling basket. Grill, turning frequently, for 45 minutes, until medium-well done.

Note: If you want to keep ducks in the freezer longer than 6 months, clean them well, and place each one in a ½ -gallon (2-liter) milk container. Fill the container with water and freeze. The containers stack nicely in the freezer, prevent freezer burn, and the duck is picture perfect for the table.

SKEWERED DUCK WITH TANGY PEANUT SAUCE

Yield: 4–6 servings

Duck, goose, sharptail, or sage grouse—this peanut sauce goes with any bird with a strong sense of self. I like my sauces tangy with strong flavors, so I use the lemon variation; if you're into hot peppers and Tabasco sauce, double the ginger.

Ingredients

5 cloves garlic, minced
1 tablespoon olive oil
2 dried red chili peppers, crushed
3 tablespoons soy sauce
½ cup (125 ml) white wine
½ cup (125 ml) peanut butter, creamy or chunky
3½ teaspoons fresh ginger root, grated
5 teaspoons coconut milk
3 tablespoons lemon juice, freshly squeezed
1 tablespoon honey
10–12 wooden skewers
2 ducks, 1 goose, or any bird with dark meat

Preparation

1. Several hours before dinner, sauté the garlic in olive oil until golden brown, then add the peppers, soy sauce, white wine, peanut butter, and only 2 teaspoons of the ginger. Stir until well blended over low heat and remove from the burner. Divide the sauce equally into two bowls.

2. **For the spicy double-ginger sauce:** In the first bowl, add the coconut milk and the rest of the ginger. Stir well.

3. **For the tangy lemon variation:** In the second bowl, add the lemon juice and honey. Stir that mixture well, too. Then put both in the refrigerator, covered, until well chilled.

Cooking

1. Start the grill, then put at least 10–12 wooden skewers in a long shallow dish and cover them with water. While the coals heat up and the skewers soak, breast out the ducks and cut the meat into strips ¼ inch (½ cm) thick by 1 inch (2½ cm) wide. Run the skewer through the length of the strips.

2. To cook as an appetizer, set the meat on the grill when the coals are not quite ready for the main course, and cook until rare. For the main course, wait until the coals are white hot, and cook the meat 5–8 minutes to a side.

3. To serve, remove the strips from the skewers and dip in the well-chilled peanut sauces.

Mallards flushing at sunrise (Photo by Erwin and Peggy Bauer)

HOT AND DIRTY DUCK ROAST

Yield: 2 servings

The two most important ingredients for this recipe are a self-cleaning oven and a large stand of chokecherry bushes. Chokecherry grows in every state of the union—but you can substitute whole cranberry sauce if you don't have access to the real thing. As for the self-cleaning oven: the only substitute is a can of industrial-grade oven cleaner.

Ingredients

1 duck, whole, plucked
Olive oil
Pepper, to taste
2 cloves garlic, minced
2 tablespoons butter
¼ cup (60 ml) dry red wine
¼ cup (60 ml) chokecherry jelly

Cooking

1. Preheat the oven on as high a setting as it goes: 500–550°F (260–290°C). Rub the duck down with olive oil, and grate black pepper over the top and inside the body cavity. Don't stuff it.

2. Place the duck in the center of the oven, breast side up. Small ducks and teal will take 15 minutes; medium, such as widgeon and golden eye, 20–25 minutes; large ducks, such as mallard, pintail, and canvasback, 25–30 minutes.

3. While the duck roasts, make the chokecherry sauce by lightly sautéing the garlic in butter and then adding the red wine. Bring the mixture to a gentle simmer and add the jelly. Simmer until the jelly has completely liquefied. Keep warm.

4. The duck will be done when you stick it with a fork and the juices run pink. Carve, and serve with the chokecherry sauce.

HEAVENLY GOOSE BREASTS

Yield: 4–6 servings

Here's the fastest recipe I've ever found for goose.

Ingredients

1 clove garlic, minced
2 tablespoons fresh ginger root, grated
Teriyaki sauce
2 goose breasts

Preparation

1. Combine garlic and ginger in a bowl and pour on enough Teriyaki sauce to cover. Marinate in the refrigerator for 1 hour.

2. When you're ready to eat, remove the breasts from the marinade, drain, and broil quickly under a hot broiler until the juice runs dark red. You can slice the meat into long slivers and serve it as an hors d'oeuvre or bring it whole to the dinner table, on a bed of wild rice.

UNSTUFFED CLAY GOOSE

Yield: 4–6 servings

I broke a clay cooker once by breaking rule #2: Don't preheat the oven. But I went out and bought another one right away, because moist heat is the best way to cook wild birds, and clay pots are the moistest way to roast a whole bird. The Unstuffed Goose is as easy as it gets—even if you do have to water the pot first. That's rule #1.

The moral of the story is to read your clay cooker directions carefully: Water the pot, put it in a cold oven, and when you take the finished bird out of the oven, place the pot on a wooden cutting board or a folded bath towel.

Ingredients

2 tart apples

1 tablespoon curry powder

1 lesser Canada goose, 3½ pounds (1½ kg); for a greater Canada goose, double the ingredients

3 toothpicks

1 teaspoon curry powder

½ cup (125 ml) lingonberries in syrup, or canned whole cranberry sauce

Cooking

1. While your clay pot is soaking in water, peel and core the apples. Measure 1 teaspoon of curry into a small bowl. Roll the skinned apples in the curry, using the back of a spoon to smooth out the lumps and even up distribution. Carefully, so you don't lose all the curry powder, stuff the apples into the goose. Close up the goose with the three toothpicks: catch up the skin on one side, stretch it gently across the gap, turn, and slide the toothpick through both sides. Sprinkle the remaining curry powder over the breast; add 1 more teaspoon of curry if necessary, to get an even, light coating. Put the goose in the pot and cover.

2. Place the water-soaked pot in the center of a *cold* oven. Cook at 450°F (230°C) for 85 minutes for a rare, 3½-pound (1½-kg) bird. Wild birds are safe to eat rare. Cook larger birds about 10 minutes longer per pound; commercially raised birds to medium or until all the pink is gone. When in doubt use a meat thermometer: a medium-done bird should register 185°F (85°C); minimum cooking should be to

170°F (76°C).

3. Remove the pot from the stove when done and place on a wooden cutting board or folded towels.

4. De-fat the juices and pour in a blender or processor. Remove the apples from the goose and add them to the blender along with 1 teaspoon of curry powder. Purée. Put the puréed mixture in a saucepan, add the lingonberries, and heat until just boiling, stirring often. If you can't find lingonberries in syrup, use canned whole cranberry sauce.

5. Carve the goose, pour sauce over each slice, and serve with rice or couscous.

Unstuffed Clay Goose (Photo by Eileen Clarke)

TRADITIONAL ROAST GOOSE

Yield: 6–8 servings

At Thanksgiving, I make both a goose and a turkey. I like to cover the goose with a piece of cheesecloth that has been soaked in melted bacon grease. During the basting process, the cheesecloth picks up all the good flavors. At the end of cooking, I take the cloth and soak it in the orange juice and then squeeze it into the gravy.

Ingredients

1 wild goose, 7–9 pounds (3–4 kg)
2 tablespoons bacon grease
$\frac{1}{2}$ medium onion, minced
1 cup (250 ml) minced celery
$\frac{1}{4}$ pound (100 ml) butter
$\frac{1}{2}$ cup (125 ml) Easy Breakfast Sausage
2 cups (500 ml) apples, chopped
8 cups (2 liters) bread, dried and cubed
$\frac{1}{2}$ teaspoon salt
$\frac{1}{2}$ teaspoon pepper

2 tablespoons dried parsley
$\frac{1}{2}$ teaspoon paprika
$\frac{1}{8}$ teaspoon ground sage
$\frac{1}{8}$ teaspoon ground thyme
Pinch of savory
Pinch of allspice
$\frac{1}{8}$ teaspoon ground coriander
1 tablespoon flour
5 oranges: juice 4; slice 1 thin
1 cup (250 ml) currant jelly

Preparation

1. Measure out a piece of cheesecloth that will cover the top of the goose completely. Melt the bacon grease in a small pot and soak the cloth in it.
2. Preheat oven to 325°F (160°C).

Cooking

1. For the stuffing: In a large skillet, sauté the onion and celery in butter; when the vegetables are soft, add the sausage and continue cooking until the sausage is browned. Stir in the apples and bread cubes, and season with salt, pepper, 1 tablespoon of the parsley, and the paprika. Stuff the goose loosely and truss with skewers and string.
2. Place the goose, breast up, on a rack in an open roasting pan, and liberally sprinkle the outside with sage, thyme, savory, allspice, coriander, and the rest of the parsley.
3. Now cover the goose with the bacon-soaked cheesecloth. Roast the goose, covered, until done, 20–25 minutes per 1 pound ($\frac{1}{2}$ kg) stuffed. When in doubt use a meat thermometer: 170–185°D (76–85°C) is rare to medium. Add a little water at the end to give some moisture to the pan.
4. Remove the goose from the roaster for carving. Remove any grease from the drippings. Dissolve 1 tablespoon flour in a small amount of water and add to the drippings. Heat until thickened, then add the orange juice. Season to taste with salt and pepper.
5. Just before serving, liquify the currant jelly into the simmering gravy. Garnish the serving platter with the orange slices.

STUFFED WILD TURKEY

Yield: 8–12 servings

Like the wild goose, wild turkeys have less fat than the domestic version and require more basting to keep the meat moist.

Ingredients

1 turkey
2 celery stalks, coarsely chopped
2 cups (500 ml) water
1½ cups (375 ml) minced celery
½ cup (125 ml) minced onions
¾ cup (185 ml) butter or margarine
16 cups (4 liters) dried and cubed bread
1 tablespoon parsley
¼ teaspoon salt
¼ teaspoon pepper
¾ teaspoon sage

⅛ teaspoon powdered thyme
Pinch of savory
Pinch of allspice
1 teaspoon paprika
3 slices bacon
½ cup (125 ml) white wine
2 tablespoons flour
3 tablespoons water
Salt and pepper, to taste

Preparation

1. Remove the neck and clean the giblets. Place the neck and giblets in a medium-size sauce pan with the celery and water, and simmer for 1 hour. Remove the giblets to cool, reserving the liquid for basting. When cooled, grate the giblets on the coarse cheese grater. Set aside. Dip the neck in a little cooking liquid and eat to keep your strength up.

2. Preheat oven to 325°F (160°C).

Cooking

1. In a large skillet, sauté the celery and onions in ½ cup (125 ml) of the butter, until translucent. Add the bread cubes, parsley, salt, pepper, ¼ teaspoon sage, thyme, savory, allspice, and ½ teaspoon of the paprika; sprinkle the grated giblets over the top and stir to blend. Place the stuffing loosely into the turkey cavity and truss with skewers and string. If everyone else isn't out hunting, have someone hold the legs for you.

2. Place the turkey, breast up, on a rack in an open roasting pan, and liberally sprinkle the body with the salt, pepper, and the remaining paprika and sage. Put the bacon slices over the breast and legs. Insert a meat thermometer into the thigh and cover the bird with a piece of tinfoil, or (as with the goose recipe above) a piece of cheesecloth soaked in ¼ cup (60 ml) butter.

3. Roast until the meat thermometer reads 170–185°F (76–85°C) or 20–25 minutes per 1 pound (½ kg) of stuffed bird. Baste frequently with the reserved liquid and wine.

4. Remove the turkey from the roaster and let it sit 15 minutes for easier carving. While it sits, first remove the stuffing, then start the gravy: Blend the flour with the water and add it slowly to the juices in the roaster, cooking over medium heat until thickened. Correct seasonings if necessary.

5. Serve with your family's traditional holiday fixings.

Eastern wild turkey tom (Photo by Erwin and Peggy Bauer)

OSCEOLA LEMON TURKEY

Yield: 8–12 servings

Jim Conley, one of the few Osceola turkey guides left in Florida, prepared this dish one morning before we left for a hunt in a mosquito-infested swamp. After a morning of watching those gangly, wise-acre Osceola turkeys—and dousing ourselves with almost enough insect repellent to prevent being sucked to death by Florida's *Mosquitus vampirus*—we walked into the lodge and got hit in the face with the most delicious aroma I've ever smelled. Osceola Lemon Turkey. It is not only the perfect reward, but it's there when you need it.

Ingredients

1 Osceola turkey; Merriam's, Rio Grande, or Eastern will do

Lemon juice (not lemonade)

3 tablespoons dried oregano, or more to taste

5–6 cloves garlic, whole

Cooking

1. Preheat oven to 300°F (150°C). The only hard part about this dish is getting enough lemon juice into the pan. You'll need about 8 ounces of juice per 1 pound of bird (225 g juice per ½ kg of bird), or a good 1–2 inches (2½–5 cm) in the bottom of the roaster. Jim likes to use bottled lemon juice; you can use fresh squeezed if you want. And don't skimp on the oregano.

2. Put the turkey and garlic in a covered roasting pan; put in the oven and go hunting. Or sit on the couch and watch a football game.

3. After about 2½ hours, boil up some potatoes and make a salad. The turkey will be done about the time the potatoes are fork tender.

SMALL GAME

RABBIT TARRAGON

Yield: 4 servings

This is a simple way of preparing cottontail or any tender rabbit. Just sauté the meat in butter and then simmer 20 minutes on the stove.

Ingredients
¼ cup (60 ml) flour
Salt and pepper, to taste
1 rabbit, cut into serving pieces
2 tablespoons butter
1 teaspoon tarragon leaves
¾ cup (185 ml) white wine

Cooking
1. Place flour, salt, and pepper in a paper bag. Add and shake the rabbit pieces, until well coated. In a Dutch oven, brown the rabbit pieces in butter, about 10 minutes.
2. When evenly browned, sprinkle the tarragon on top and add the wine. Cover and simmer over low heat for 20 minutes more or until the meat is tender.
3. Serve straight out of the pot or place on a serving platter with carrots and potatoes.

DEEP FRIED RABBIT

Yield: 4 servings

I have to be truthful on this one: I had a lot of friends who wouldn't eat any wild meat. So one night, I served fried chicken *and* fried rabbit, and didn't say anything. All my non–game-eating friends preferred the juiciness of the rabbit.

Ingredients
1 cup (250 ml) flour
1½ teaspoons baking powder
2 teaspoons sugar
½ teaspoon salt
¼ teaspoon paprika
⅛ teaspoon pepper
⅛ teaspoon sage
⅛ teaspoon thyme
⅛ teaspoon powdered coriander
Pinch of savory
Pinch of allspice
1 egg, separated
¾ cup (185 ml) milk
Cooking oil
1 cottontail rabbit, cut into pieces

Cooking
1. Combine the flour, baking soda, sugar, and seasonings; add the egg yolk and enough milk to make a thick batter. Beat the egg white until stiff, and fold in.
2. In a deep fat fryer, heat the oil to 350°F (175°C). Dip the rabbit pieces into the batter, letting the excess drip back into the bowl. Then carefully place the pieces into the oil one at a time. Do this slowly to maintain the cooking temperature of the oil.
2. Cook about 10 minutes, or until the pieces turn a rich golden brown on the outside, and the juices run clear. Serve with mashed potatoes and peas.

HASENPFEFFER

Yield: 4–6 servings

This was another German dish that was passed along in the Strung household. If you are uncertain of the tenderness of Bugs, or if you're using jackrabbit or hare, the marinating and the cooking process will surely tenderize him.

Marinade Ingredients
1½ cups (375 ml) cider vinegar
1½ cups (375 ml) water
2 onions, sliced
1 tablespoon sugar
2 teaspoons salt
¼ teaspoon peppercorns
½ teaspoon crumbled cinnamon stick
5 whole cloves
1 bay leaf
¼ teaspoon chilies, crushed

Hasenpfeffer Ingredients
2 rabbits, cut into serving pieces
¼ cup (60 ml) plus 2 tablespoons flour
Salt and pepper, to taste
3 tablespoons butter
¼ cup (60 ml) water

Mountain cottontail (Photo by Erwin and Peggy Bauer)

Preparation
1. Blend together a marinade of vinegar, water, onions, sugar, salt, peppercorns, cinnamon, cloves, bay leaf, and chilies. Place the rabbit in a large bowl and cover with the marinade. Cover with plastic wrap, and let stand in the refrigerator for 24 hours or more, turning the meat occasionally.
2. Remove the rabbit and dry with a paper towel. Place ¼ cup (60 ml) of the flour in a paper bag and season with the salt and pepper. Shake the pieces in the bag to cover with flour mixture.

Cooking
1. Heat the butter in a heavy skillet, and brown the rabbit over a medium heat. Strain the marinade, and add it to the meat, then cover and simmer for about 1 hour or until fork tender. Transfer the rabbit to a warm serving platter.
2. Mix the 2 tablespoons of flour and the water, and add to the pan juices to make a thick gravy. Serve with buttered noodles.

JUGGED HARE

Yield: 4 servings

Most people in my neck of the woods look at you with a jaundiced eye if you waste your time hunting cottontails. I don't even want to admit that I take jackrabbits home. But if you marinate them a day or two, and cook them for 5–6 hours, and do it in a pseudo-traditional, semi-English way, jackrabbits are highly acceptable table fare.

Marinade Ingredients

1 jackrabbit, jointed; save the liver and heart
1 cup (250 ml) dry red wine (or rabbit blood, which is traditional)

Cooking Ingredients

1 large onion, coarsely chopped
1 carrot
½ cup (125 ml) flour
4½ tablespoons butter or margarine
½ pound (250 g) bacon, chopped into ½-inch (1-cm) squares
1–2 shallots, sliced in rings
1 celery stalk, chopped
¼ pound (100 ml) mushrooms, sliced (more to taste)
3 cups stock
¼ teaspoon powdered mace
¼ teaspoon cloves
Bouquet garni: 5 sprigs parsley, 3 sprigs thyme, 1 bay leaf
1 clove garlic, minced
juice of 1 lemon
2 strips of lemon rind
Port to taste
2 tablespoons currant jelly
Brown sugar to taste

Preparation

1. Marinate the jointed rabbit for at least 24 hours in red wine, turning occasionally.
2. Put a few venison bones into a pot with enough water to cover, onion, and 1 carrot, and let it simmer 2–3 hours. Drain the broth and reserve.

Cooking

1. Dry the rabbit thoroughly, then dust with ½ cup (125 ml) flour. In a large skillet, brown the rabbit in 3 tablespoons of butter. Remove the meat to a Dutch oven or covered roaster.
2. Add the bacon to the skillet and fry until a good bit of the fat appears, then push the bacon to one side and add the onion, shallots, celery, and mushrooms. Brown until they are limp, then add to the rabbit pot. Cut up the liver and heart, and brown them too, adding them to the rabbit pot when done.
3. Preheat oven to 350°F (175°C). Heat up the stock. Add mace, cloves, bouquet garni, garlic, and the lemon juice and rind. Stir to distribute the rabbit evenly, and cover it in the sauce. Cover and place in the oven and cook for 2 hours. Then, turn the heat down to 225°F (110°C) for at least 3 more hours. Check occasionally; if the rabbit is getting dry, add more stock or wine.
4. When the rabbit is falling off the bones, remove it from the pot and keep warm. Discard the bouquet garni. Put the pot on the stovetop over low heat and stir in the remaining butter and flour, which has been thoroughly mixed. Add port to taste and stir, but do not let the pot boil. Add jelly and keep stirring. Add brown sugar if necessary and keep stirring until the sauce is smooth.
5. Pour the sauce over the rabbit, and serve with mashed potatoes, French bread, and dry red wine.

RABBIT AND MUSTARD STEW

Yield: 4–6 servings

This is a recipe from the Irish, but made with cottontail instead of hare, which means instead of an overnight marinade, followed by a couple of hours in the pot, it cooks up in 30 minutes or less. You could also substitute any bird with light meat for the rabbit.

Colman's English Mustard is a finely ground, mild mustard available even in Montana grocery stores.

Ingredients

2 tablespoons bacon fat or butter
1 large onion, sliced
1 cottontail rabbit, diced into 1–2-inch (2½–5-cm) pieces
4–6 tablespoons flour
3 cups (750 ml) stock, or chicken broth
2 cups (500 ml) carrots, diced
1 tablespoon Colman's English Mustard
1 dozen parsley stalks, leaves and all, tied together
1 teaspoon leaf thyme
Pepper, to taste
2 bay leaves
⅓ cup (80 ml) cream
2 tablespoons dried parsley

Cooking

1. Heat bacon fat (or butter) in a large pot or Dutch oven and sauté the onion until soft. Push the onion to one side and brown the rabbit.
2. Stir in the flour and mix thoroughly. The mix will be dry at this point. Now add the stock or bouillon, stirring well to pick up the flour. Add the carrots, mustard, parsley stalks, and seasonings, and bring to a boil. Then turn down to a gentle simmer and cook about 15–25 minutes, until the carrots are tender.
3. Just before serving, throw out the parsley stalks, add the cream, stirring until well blended, and sprinkle the dried parsley over the top. Serve over rice.

SQUIRREL IN ONION SAUCE

Yield: 2–4 servings

This recipe comes from a friend who loves to sit on his back porch with his .22 rifle.

Ingredients

2 tablespoons butter
¼ cup (60 ml) brandy
1 tablespoon parsley, dried
2 cups (500 ml) chopped onions
2 tomatoes, sliced thin
3 cloves garlic, minced
2 squirrels, cut in pieces
2 cups (500 ml) water
Salt and pepper, to taste

Cooking

1. In a medium-size sauce pan, melt the butter over very low heat and add the brandy, parsley, onions, tomatoes, and garlic, and simmer, covered, for 15 minutes. The onions should be limp.
2. Add the squirrel pieces and water, and cook, uncovered, until tender, about 45 minutes. Season to taste with salt and pepper.

FISH

The Power of Fishing

When it gets hot in Montana, it gets hot and dry. The humidity drops down to single digits and the dust starts blowing so it's everywhere: it sifts into the windows, over the door sills, in your hair, and in your food. The grasshoppers grow wings so they can find more food and formerly sane people start praying for winter. That's when I grab my short fly rod, throw on some jeans and a long-sleeved shirt, and load up the cooler with sandwiches and pop. Forty-five miles from my house, on the other side of the Missouri River, there's a mountain range made of basalt and limestone, with snow-capped peaks ten months of the year, and a tiny creek that winds down the mountain through caverns and rockface,

Fly fishing at dawn in Wyoming (Photo by Erwin and Peggy Bauer)

zen, disked farmland and having the birds flush wild out of range. Or freezing in a duck blind, whitetail stand, or being blown off the antelope prairie by gusts of wind. Fishing is fun. You don't need to call your six closest friends to help you haul your creel out of the woods; you don't need to knock on doors to ask permission. You can fish with worms, corn, cheese, garlic-flavored marshmallows, rubber newts, roe, artificial flies, gaudy orange and yellow plastic bobbers; you can fish in metallic flaked speedboats, birch bark, wood, or fiberglass canoes, camouflage-painted Styrofoam rings, $300 inner tubes or $5,000 wheel chairs, or wade wet in a pair of old sneakers. A five-year-old can pull sunfish from a city pond with a Donald Duck

boulders and towering pines. We wade wet, letting the jeans and shirt sleeves protect our skin from the rough limestone and wild roses, and the stupid little trout who live here restore our souls. That's what fishing is—in summer.

In winter, it's my friend Bill Sorber packing up his ice fishing auger, fishing rods, and a warm jacket, and ice skating out onto a Pennsylvania Lake. He cuts four holes at three-hundred-yard (285-m) intervals and ice skates in lazy-eights, checking his lines all afternoon. My friend Mike Fogt bought a house on Florida's inland waterway and has a dock—and his saltwater boat—down the garden path from his back door. Take a trip with any of us on a down-in-the-dumps day— saltwater, freshwater, or frozen water—and we'll show you what fishing is. Starting by telling you what it isn't.

It isn't elk hunting—as much as I love elk—walking around the woods all hunting season and maybe cutting a track once in a while. It isn't bird hunting— as much as I love birds—tripping over clumps of fro-

foldable rod while Mom takes photos with a disposable camera, or you can hand down cane fly rods from father to son, mother to daughter, and fly bay to bay in a Twin Otter fishing for lunker salmon.

I prefer small streams, fresh from the mountains and not yet slowed down to warm, snaky plains streams. Creeks with deep holes and dead willows hanging over them; holes that eat four out of five flies and then— maybe—reward you with a rise. (A wide yellow flash that says, "Not good enough yet, Honey.") Rivers where thunderstorms fall down from the mountains at blazing speeds, leaving you looking over your shoulder to get one more cast in before you run for the truck and try to beat it to town. Water no one else bothers to fish because it's too hard, too far, not on anyone's Honey Hole map, and the fish are too small and too stupid to be "challenging." Sorry, that's what I like best. The challenge isn't in the fish. It's in the day, the season, the rocks, and the sun. Anyone can find smart fish: just go to the heavily fished places—places where the fish have pin cushions for lips.

Previous page: *Rainbow trout (Photo by Sil Strung)*

There's a story about a fisherman who dies and when he wakes up, he's standing in a trout stream with a three-pound (1½-kg) trout on his line. He releases that one, and another just like the last gives him a tug. And another and another. Finally, he turns to his guide—maybe this is less a story about fishing than about a guy who assumes there'd be a guide—and says, "Boy, if this is heaven, you'd think they'd vary the size of the fish." And the man answers, "Who said this is heaven?"

I don't want the wily trout. What I want is to learn the pattern of the stream. And while only a few people can afford to always fish the "hot" places, the Blue Ribbon Streams, and be the first western angler to float Siberia, anyone can learn their own backyard stream. To me that's the pleasure of fishing.

In that sense, fishing is as democratic as sport comes. No matter how we approach it, we are all faced with that same impenetrable surface: the top of the water. Computers can give us a vague picture of objects below, but the world underneath the surface of the water has been alien to *Homo erectus* since amphibians first crawled onto dry land. I have a friend who spent most of his teenage summers snorkeling on a spring creek. But I think even he would admit it ain't instinct; it's being out there summer, winter, fall, and spring, in all weather, all moods; knowing the stream through feast and famine, above and below the surface as well as the rise and fall of yearly precipitation that makes us successful. And sheer luck. But it's not luck that brings the fish to the back door prime for cooking. There's no magic, impenetrable truth. Carry a creel, wet it down good, and as soon as possible put the fish on ice. Simple, but I'd guess only 50 percent of all caught fish get treated like that.

I used to live a couple miles down the road from a bucket-o'-fish guy named Randy. One hot sunny day I stopped at the local bar. Meredith, the owner/operator, was a character of monumental proportions, and once in the bar, I sat and had a glass of iced tea with her. Randy was down at the end of the bar, and Meredith made an off-hand comment that he'd been down there for a couple of hours. She wasn't too pleased about that, but, as usual didn't have long to wait for one of her regulars to come in and roust old Randy. Dick was a trucker, usually off hauling wheat or cattle. But when he walked in that day, he was loaded for bear. He walked straight down the bar, pulled Randy off his barstool and told him that if he ever fished at his pond again, he'd beat him to a pulp. Meredith asked Dick what he was harassing Randy for—not that she was going to stop him. She was just nosy.

"He's been sitting here minding his business since I opened the place," she said.

"He's got a bucket of fish sitting in his pickup. In the sun. Off of my kid pond." His kid pond wasn't just for his kids; he planted it each year in rainbow trout for all the kids in town. Randy had a bucket of four-pounders and no kid in sight. Randy perched back up on the barstool and looked Dick right in the eye. "I'm gonna find 'em homes soon as I'm done here."

"And gut 'em," Dick added.

"Whoever eats them can gut them. They'll be fine until then," Randy shot back.

I've met other people who believed that. Two people I met later, separately, were carrying dead trout on a stringer from spot to spot. When I asked if they had a creel, they each told me that fish don't go bad until you gut them. You can carry them around all day, they told me, as long as you don't gut them. I don't know where this stuff comes from, but it sounds a lot like folks who buy a truck and don't figure in the cost of tires. ("Let's see, we'll pay for the tranny, and a 416 engine—gotta go—and maybe brakes—gotta stop—radio, tape deck. Yup. Tires? Gee, got no money left for tires.") But at least those dead fish were past caring. The most outrageous thing I've ever heard is that the best way to keep a live fish healthy is on a stringer, back in the water it came from. Wrong. Delicate fish like trout and bass will get bruised fighting the stringer; and if they die anyway while they're on the stringer, warm water—like bass habitat—allows bacterial growth.

Here are a few simple rules:

1. As soon as you catch the fish it starts going downhill. Carry a creel, keep it wet, and ice it as soon as possible. If you're fishing from a boat, carry a cooler of ice just for fish.

2. Any fish you keep should be killed immediately and gutted as soon as possible—including removing the long red line (the kidneys) on either side of the spine—and rinsed in clean water. Then put it on ice for the ride home, if it isn't iced already.

3. Once home, cook or freeze the fish as soon as pos-

sible. Oily fish like salmon and trout, particularly lake trout and char, will turn on you faster than less-oily fish like walleye, pike, and bass. Still, all fish are better fresh.

4. To freeze fish, use a vacuum pack or a zip-lock bag and carefully press out all the air. If you catch a lot of small fish, freeze them in milk cartons—essentially in a block of ice.

And what if you're about to take the trip of a lifetime—fishing for Alaskan salmon or Arctic char—and want to bring some of the catch home? Here are a couple more rules:

1. Most fishing lodges will fillet and freeze your catch, and even provide you with an insulated cardboard box to get them back on the plane. But call ahead, and check to make sure these services are offered.

2. The second choice is to bring the fish back in a soft or hard cooler. The airlines allow four pieces of luggage in the form of two check-in and two carry-on bags. Plan on counting the cooler as your second check-in on the return trip, or paying the airline for an extra bag. The advantage of the soft cooler is that you can stuff it in your other check-in on the way out. Either way, bring duct tape to secure the cooler.

So before you go out there with malice aforethought and rod in hand, be prepared. There's nothing like a sudden tug on the other end of the line on a hot sweaty day; ice skating on the topmost door of Perch World; or just blowing off the hustle and bustle of south Florida, from the galloping subdivisions to the carnivorous mosquitoes, and heading out to the ocean for a day of fishing. Give me a minute of fishing for every hour of work and I will die a happy woman; one second for every hot August wind. Who says there's no heaven on earth? But do what you can to deserve it: take care of the catch.

The Basics of Small Trout

If the world were an ideal place, we would go fishing with a fry pan instead of a net and have a fire going before we ever wet the line. That's the way they taste best. From there, all the variations grow.

Put the fish in the pan naked or roll it in a variety of processed grains from flour and corn meal to breakfast cereals like corn flakes—the Irish even use oatmeal sometimes and perhaps the Germans use hops in a pinch. You can wet the fish first, with stream water, tap water, beer, milk, or egg. Or put all the above together and make a batter, Japanese-style for tempura or Milwaukee-style with beer. Deep fry it in lard, pan fry it in olive oil, or sauté in a whisper of butter. Poach it in a Dutch oven, or go to a serious kitchen store and buy an elongated silver pan that does nothing else but cook fish in what is regally called Court Bouillon. Or carry a fish-shaped grate in your back pocket, clamp the fish on, and grill it over an open fire. Throw catsup on it, or Tabasco; mustard or tartar sauce. Nuke it, shred it, sauce it and put it between two slices of bread. Cook it with hash browns in the morning, French fries for lunch, crumpets for tea, and herbed potatoes for dinner.

But don't overcook it. Use the general rule of 10 minutes per inch ($2\frac{1}{2}$ cm) at the thickest part. Don't abuse it: kill and clean it immediately, carry it in a wet creel, and get it on ice—chipped ice preferably, or cubes—within 2 hours. Take only enough to eat that day, but keep the first one to be sure you'll eat. And some day, when you have nothing pressing to come home to—or better yet, when you do—cut a forked willow and cook the fish Paul Bunyan style. You may find that trout tastes even better without walls.

Here are some more specific recipes for fish of all sizes, but starting out small.

FRESHWATER FISH AND SALMON

MICROWAVE TROUT SALAD

Yield: 1 serving

So you like tuna salad and like to fish, too? Next time you catch a small trout, make your own fish salad. You won't have to worry about the porpoises, or gill nets, and since you cook in the microwave, you can fix it on a hot sultry day and not sweat up the kitchen.

Ingredients
1 tiny trout
1 tablespoon chopped onion
1 tablespoon sweet pickle or fresh cucumber
Mayonnaise to moisten
Salt and pepper, to taste

Cooking
1. Clean the trout and wrap it in a paper towel. Microwave on high for 30 seconds. Test it: If you can't take a butter knife and slide the meat off the bones, it's not done. Microwave a few seconds more—but be careful, small trout nuke fast.
2. When the meat slides easily off the bones, remove all the meat. It will come off in bite-sized pieces. Set it aside.
3. Depending on the size of the fish, and your personal taste, dice enough onion and cucumber (pickled or not) to suit you. Then add the fish to the onion mixture and enough mayonnaise to moisten. Salt and pepper to taste. Serve on a bed of lettuce, two slices of bread, or crackers.

Note: You can substitute non-fat yogurt for almost all the mayo: The yogurt takes on the flavor of mayo very easily. Over the years I've decreased the ratio of mayonnaise to yogurt until I put in only a dab of mayo. All the flavor, little of the fat.

Fly fishing in the Beartooth Mountains of Montana (Photo by Erwin and Peggy Bauer)

POACHED TROUT

Yield: 2–4 servings

For most hunters, *poaching* is a nasty word. But for an angler, poaching is a delicious way to bring trout to the table with no added fat. Buy a poacher at a serious kitchen store—they start at 18 inches (48 cm) in size—or fillet the fish and poach it in a Dutch oven, or even put it in a roasting pan and curve the fish to fit.

Ingredients
Dry white wine to cover the fish
1 bay leaf
1 teaspoon ground cumin
1 trout, 15–18 inch (37–45 cm), whole
½ cup (125 ml) butter
1 tablespoon lemon juice, freshly squeezed

Cooking
1. Put wine, bay leaf, and cumin in the poacher, bring to a boil, and simmer several minutes until the water turns slightly brown and the spices release their flavor. You can mix 1 cup (250 ml) white wine with water to cover; but the more wine you use the better the fish. Reduce the heat until it is just below a simmer: the water will shimmer but not bubble. If you're not using a poacher with a removable grate, wrap the fish in muslin to make for easier retrieval.

2. Place the fish in the poacher, check to see that the liquid covers the fish and keep the water at a simmer. (Letting it come to a bubbling boil will break up the fish.) Cooking time varies: use the 10 minutes per 1 inch (2½ cm) of thickness rule, and check with a meat thermometer. It will be ready when the thermometer hits 150°F (65°C) and when the meat is opaque rather than translucent.

3. As the fish nears completion, melt the butter in a saucepan and add the lemon juice. Dip the fish in the lemon sauce, or pour the sauce over each serving.

BLUED TROUT

Yield: one 10-inch (25-cm) trout per person

To blue a trout properly you should have a freshly killed fish, about 10 inches (25 cm) in length. Brookies blue up the best, but any trout will do. The secret is to add vinegar to the cooking liquid; it interacts with that slimy film on newly killed trout. But the more you handle the fish, the less it will blue.

Ingredients
3 cups (750 ml) water
½ cup (125 ml) white vinegar
½ cup (125 ml) dry white wine
1 small onion, sliced thin
4 peppercorns
2 cloves
½ teaspoon salt
1 bay leaf
½ lemon, juiced
1 10-inch (25-cm) trout

Cooking
1. Combine water, vinegar, wine, onion, spices, and lemon juice in a large shallow pan and bring to a rolling boil. Holding the fish by the tail, gently lower it into the water, then bring the water back to a boil.

2. Turn the heat down to simmer and cook, uncovered, until the trout turns a pale blue and the meat pulls easily from the bone, about 5–7 minutes.

GRILLED FISH STEAKS

Yield: 2 servings

As you can tell by some of the recipes, I like to use a hinged grate for barbecuing. It makes life much simpler: Fish don't fall into the fire, and you can put the whole meal on one grate and cook it up at once.

Grilled Fish Steaks (Photo by Sil Strung)

Ingredients

1 pound (½ kg) of fish steaks (salmon, pike, walleye)

½ teaspoon soy sauce

¼ cup (60 ml) prepared mustard

¼ cup (60 ml) mayonnaise

Cooking

1. Pre-heat barbecue on high for 10 minutes; turn down to medium.

2. Brush both sides of the steaks with soy sauce; then combine mustard and mayonnaise and brush that on the steaks.

3. Grill 5 minutes to a side, or until you can flake it with a fork.

Fish steaks ready for the grill (Photo by Sil Strung)

Trout in Foil

Yield: 4–6 servings

This recipe can be used outside on the barbecue, in camp over charcoals, or at home in the oven.

Trout in Foil (Photo by Sil Strung)

Ingredients

2–3 trout
1 teaspoon butter or margarine
1 teaspoon lemon juice
¼ teaspoon garlic powder
½ teaspoon dried parsley
Salt and pepper, to taste
1 onion, thinly sliced
1 tomato, thinly sliced
¼ green pepper, thinly sliced
½ cup (125 ml) white wine or dry vermouth

Preparation

1. Preheat propane barbecue to medium heat, or preheat oven to 350°F (175°C).
2. Place the fish on a piece of aluminum foil, folding the foil into a rectangular boat to keep the fluids from dripping out. Smear the fish cavity with butter, then sprinkle inside and out with the lemon juice, garlic, parsley, salt, and pepper. Lay the slices of onion, tomatoes, and pepper on top and pour the wine around the fish.
3. Seal the aluminum foil, leaving a little bit of space at the top for the steam to escape. Place the fish on the grill or in the oven. Cook 10 minutes for each 1 inch (2½ cm) of thickness. Watch carefully: The fish is done when the meat pulls easily from the bone with a fork, and it is opaque.

BEER BATTER FISH

Yield: 2–4 servings

Any fish fillet, or even small whole fish, will work and the batter seals the moisture in.

Ingredients

1 cup (250 ml) flour
1 cup (250 ml) beer
2 tablespoons baking powder
1 teaspoon sugar
½ teaspoon table salt
¼ teaspoon paprika
1 pound (½ kg) fish fillet
3 cups (750 ml) canola oil

Cooking

1. Make the batter by combining the flour, beer, baking powder, sugar, salt, and paprika, and mix until just moistened. The batter will be very thick. Set aside.

2. Heat the skillet to hot but not smoking. Dip the fish, two or three pieces at a time, in the batter and then into hot oil. Cook until browned on both sides, turning once. Place on a paper towel to absorb the grease, and then into a 200°F (95°C) oven to keep warm.

3. Repeat this process until all the fish are fried. Do not put all the pieces in the oil at the same time—they will cool the grease down and the fish will not cook properly.

4. Serve with coleslaw and Cajun Corn.

Bass fishing in Louisiana (Photo by Erwin and Peggy Bauer)

TEMPURA FRIED FISH

Yield: 2–4 servings

My friend Paul is an avid ice fisherman, and one dark, nasty February day, he brought a bread sack full of perch to our house, dug out our deep fat fryer, and started making tempura. We came downstairs to the aroma of a delicious—and free—dinner.

Ingredients
1 cup (250 ml) flour
1 cup (250 ml) ice cold water
½ teaspoon salt
½ teaspoon sugar
1 egg, slightly beaten
2 teaspoons vegetable oil
3–6 cups (750–1500 ml) fat for the deep fat fryer
1 pound (½ kg) fish fillets, in 1-inch (2½-cm) cubes

Cooking
1. Combine flour, water, salt, sugar, egg, and oil; stir lightly. The batter will be thick. Keep cold by placing the batter bowl into a larger bowl of ice. Turn the deep fat fryer to 375°F (190°C).
2. Dip fish into the batter, one piece at a time, letting the excess batter drip back into the bowl. Gently slide coated fish into the hot fat and cook until coating is a rich brown. The fish should be flaky when you bite into it.
3. Serve with a chilled tartar sauce made of ½ cup (125 ml) mayonnaise and 1 tablespoon relish.

CRISPY TROUT

Yield: 4–6 servings

We used to go camping and fishing with a large group of friends. Inevitably someone would catch too many fish to eat that day. We tried to keep these fish on ice, but they would soon become soft. So here's a good way to make soft fish taste great.

Ingredients
2 pounds (1 kg) soft fish
1 egg, slightly beaten
½ cup (125 ml) milk
½ cup (125 ml) cracker crumbs
½ cup (125 ml) cornmeal
½ teaspoon salt
½ teaspoon pepper
½ teaspoon garlic salt
½ teaspoon oregano
1 tablespoon dried parsley
Cooking oil, ½ inch (1 cm) deep in frying pan

Cooking
1. Fillet the fish, then tear meat into 3-inch (7½-cm) lengths. Combine the egg and milk, mix well. Combine the cracker crumbs, cornmeal, and seasonings in a plastic bread bag and shake well to mix.
2. Dip the fish in the milk mixture and, one at a time, put the trout pieces into the bag and shake to coat well. Remove from the bag and set aside to dry for a few minutes.
3. Heat the oil in a large skillet. Test with one piece of fish: The oil should bubble when the trout hits it. Fry each piece 3–5 minutes, until golden brown.
4. Serve with this quick cocktail sauce made of ½ cup (125 ml) catsup, 1 tablespoon prepared horseradish, and ½ teaspoon lemon juice. Chill if desired.

NUTTY TROUT

Trout fishing in Wyoming (Photo by Erwin and Peggy Bauer)

Yield: 2 servings

In Europe they make this trout recipe with hazelnuts because they're plentiful. If you can't find hazelnuts, use almonds, but be just as careful when browning the nuts: they both burn easily.

Ingredients

¼ cup (60 ml) flour
Salt and pepper, to taste
1 trout, 15-inch (38-cm), cleaned but whole
3 tablespoons butter
½ cup (125 ml) hazelnuts, chopped
1 teaspoon dill
1 lemon

Cooking

1. Mix the flour, salt, and pepper, and dust the trout with the mixture.
2. Melt the butter in a cast-iron skillet on medium and pan fry the trout—10 minutes per 1 inch (2½ cm) of thickness—or until you can just pull the meat from the bones.
3. Turn the broiler on. Sprinkle the almonds over the top of the trout, and slide the cast-iron pan under the broiler to brown the nuts—no more than 30 seconds.
4. To serve, sprinkle with dill and a squeeze of lemon.

CHILLED DILL TROUT

Yield: 2 servings

Chilled Dill is a low-fat sauce with lots of flavor, perfect for any fish, cooked any way, cold or hot. Here, we'll microwave a whole small trout for a delicious, chilled summer meal.

Brook trout (Photo by Sil Strung)

Ingredients

1 cup (250 ml) non-fat yogurt
2 tablespoons sour cream (or skip it if you're already a yogurt fan)
1 tablespoon dill weed, dried
1 cucumber
1 trout, 10–12-inch (25–30-cm), cleaned but whole
Salt and pepper, to taste

Preparation

1. Combine the yogurt, sour cream, and dill in a food processor. Peel and quarter the cucumber, add to the yogurt, and purée. Chill at least 3 hours; more is better to allow the dill to develop its flavor.

2. Wrap the trout in a paper towel and microwave 60 seconds on high in a 500-watt unit, 30 seconds in a 700-watt unit. Test to see if the trout is done: the meat will be opaque and come away from the spine easily. If the flesh is still translucent, microwave only 10 seconds more at a time, until almost done. Then leave in the oven, wrapped in the towel, to finish off cooking. Chill.

3. Taste the chilled sauce and add more dill if necessary; salt and pepper to taste. Now dip the cold trout into the chilled sauce or pour the sauce over cold trout. You can even eat the trout hot from the microwave, dipped in cold sauce.

LAKE TROUT STUFFED WITH CRAB MEAT

Yield: 6–8 servings

When we go to Mexico, one of our afternoon pleasures is to go out and catch some blue claw crabs. We bring them home, boil them up, and have them for dinner. But I always freeze some to bring back to Montana for the first large trout of the year.

Ingredients

¾ cup (185 ml) chopped celery
¼ cup (60 ml) chopped onions
3 tablespoons butter or margarine
8 slices bread, dried and cubed
1 teaspoon parsley
¼ teaspoon salt
¼ teaspoon pepper
1 egg, slightly beaten
1 pound (½ kg) crab meat, diced
1 tablespoon dry sherry
1 lake trout, 4 pounds (2 kg) or larger
½ teaspoon lemon juice

Cooking

1. Over medium heat, sauté the celery and onions in butter until translucent. Add the cubed bread, parsley, salt, pepper, and stir in the beaten egg. Add the crab meat, stir, and sprinkle the sherry over the top.
2. Preheat oven to 400°F (205°C). Rub the fish cavity with the lemon juice. Stuff the fish with the crab mixture and close with toothpicks. Grease a piece of foil and place the stuffed fish on it. Seal it completely.
3. Bake for 1 hour or until the meat flakes easily with a fork.

Trout on fern leaves (Photo by John Barsness)

Lake Trout on the Grill

Yield: $\frac{1}{3}$–$\frac{1}{2}$ pound (165–250 g) cleaned fish per person

After a hard day fishing, there's nothing better than sitting around the grill with six of your best friends passively watching a fire prepare your dinner as the sun goes down.

Ingredients

1 quick spray of cooking oil
1 lake trout, 6–8 pounds (2$\frac{3}{4}$–3$\frac{1}{2}$ kg), freshly caught and filleted
3 tomatoes, chopped
1 large onion, sliced and separated into rings
2–3 lemons, sliced
$\frac{1}{2}$ cup (125 ml) white wine, or more to taste
Salt and pepper, to taste

Cooking

1. Make a double layer of aluminum foil, long enough to double over the fillets and wide enough to fold the sides up into a pouch. Spray the bottom of the pouch with a light coat of oil, then place your fish fillets in the center. Add the tomato, onions, and generous slices of lemon. Add the wine, depending on the size of your fish. Sprinkle lightly with salt and pepper.

2. Fold the long sides of the foil over each other to seal. Fold the ends over twice and seal the juices in tightly.

3. Cook on a propane barbecue about 45 minutes on medium heat, or place on a cookie sheet and bake in a 350°F (175°C) oven for 25–35 minutes. Check once about halfway through the cooking. When the meat flakes and begins to separate, take it off the grill and serve with a crusty bread.

Cajun Corn

Yield: 4–6 servings

A custardy corn dish with a Cajun twang, Cajun Corn is the perfect accompaniment for steaks, roasts, or pan-fried fish. It has a bit of a bite, so if you're sensitive to pepper, cut the chili and white peppers by half, but don't leave them out completely.

Ingredients

1 large onion, diced
5 cloves garlic, minced
1 tablespoon olive oil
1 green bell pepper
3 cups (750 ml) corn
1 teaspoon white pepper
1 teaspoon dried red chili peppers, crushed
1 egg, slightly beaten
$\frac{1}{2}$ cup (125 ml) cornmeal
2 cups (500 ml) milk

Cooking

1. Preheat oven to 350°F (175°C). In a Dutch oven, sauté the onion and garlic in olive oil until slightly browned; then add the green pepper, corn (if frozen, thaw in the microwave before adding), and white and red peppers. Cook over medium heat about 4 minutes, until all the ingredients are thoroughly hot. Add the egg, cornmeal, and milk one at a time and stir well after adding each one.

2. Place the Dutch oven, uncovered in the oven and bake for 1 hour. The liquid will be absorbed and the top brown when done.

SALMON APPETIZER

Yield: 8–10 servings

For those who love pickled herring, like my husband John, here's a simple dish for salmon that makes a perfect appetizer for game dinners.

Ingredients
4 pounds (2 kg) salmon
3 pounds (1½ kg) kosher salt
2 cloves garlic, sliced
2 onions, chopped
1 bunch parsley, diced
½ cup (125 ml) olive oil
1–2 cups (250–500 ml) cooking oil
Freshly ground black pepper, to taste
2 lemons

Preparation
1. Fillet a side of salmon, then remove the skin, bones, and fat. Cut into 4–5-inch (10–12½-cm) lengths. In a shallow baking dish or storage container sprinkle a layer of salt; apply a layer of fish slabs over the salt and sprinkle salt over them. Continue layering salt, fish, salt, fish, salt until all the fish is covered with salt. Don't skimp, salt is cheap. Now cover the dish loosely with plastic wrap and put it in the refrigerator for 7 days.
2. On the seventh day, the fish will be firm, even in the middle, and chewy. Rinse the excess salt off the fish and dry well.
3. With the salmon flat on the cutting board, slice at a 45-degree angle as thin as you possibly can until all the meat is sliced up. Place it in a large bowl and add the garlic, onions, parsley, and olive oil. Add enough cooking oil to cover the fish. Empty the contents of

the bowl into the shallow baking dish and cover with plastic wrap, using the palm of your hand to press out the air pockets and your fingers to seal up the edge of the fish mixture to the sides of the container. Return to the refrigerator for 7–12 hours. Allow 24 hours before serving. (You can also vacuum seal and freeze the salted fish for several months; once the salmon is packed in oil it will keep for 2–3 weeks in the refrigerator.)
4. To serve, spoon some of the fish onto a cracker, add pepper to taste, and squeeze a bit of lemon juice over the top.

Layering salmon fillets in salt for Salmon Appetizer (Photo by Eileen Clarke)

Barbecued Salmon with Mustard Sauce

Yield: $\frac{1}{3}$–$\frac{1}{2}$ pound (165–250 g) cleaned fish per person

This is a recipe for large salmon, those hook-jawed lunkers that play you until your arms ache and you think maybe there is such a thing as catching too many fish in one day.

If you caught your own, congratulations, but if you're thinking of cooking it streamside, be sure the fish is not in *rigor mortis*—the natural stiffening occurring shortly after death. Cook it before *rigor mortis* sets in—immediately after catching—or after the fish has relaxed again. Cooking during *rigor mortis* will make a perfectly tender and fresh fish tough.

Ingredients

1 salmon, 20 pounds (9 kg) or more, whole
$\frac{1}{4}$ pound (100 ml) butter
$\frac{1}{4}$ cup (60 ml) catsup
3 tablespoons soy sauce
3 tablespoons lemon juice
2 tablespoons prepared mustard
1 clove garlic
Dash of Worcestershire sauce

Cooking

1. Wrap the salmon in foil, being careful to seal the ends, and place it on the grill over at least 4 dozen white-hot briquettes. Turn occasionally, but don't flip it every 2 minutes; all you need to do is keep the side away from the fire hot enough to keep cooking. It'll be about every 10 minutes, depending on the size of the fish.

2. While the salmon cooks, melt the butter in a saucepan and add the rest of the ingredients. Stir until the sauce is thoroughly mixed, but do not allow it to boil. Set it aside and go test the salmon.

3. The general rule for fish is 10 minutes for every 1 inch (2 $\frac{1}{2}$ cm) of thickness at the thickest part of the fish. But it's a general rule. The other general rule is that the fish is done when it flakes. The danger is to overcook; it doesn't mean when the meat falls apart on its own and becomes "flaky." That's too far. "When it flakes" means you can pull the meat from the back with a fork. Other ways to tell are that the flesh is slightly springy when it's done; there is a smell of cooked fish; and last but not least, a meat thermometer registers 150°F (65°C).

4. To serve, remove the fish from the foil and place it on a platter; pour the sauce into a serving bowl and let people help themselves.

Float fishing for salmon on the Rogue River, Oregon (Photo by Erwin and Peggy Bauer)

CURRIED SALMON

Yield: 2–3 servings

Fishing for silver salmon in Alaska (Photo by Erwin and Peggy Bauer)

This is a fast way of preparing a salmon fillet on the grill. I learned this from a friend who's always in a hurry.

Ingredients

1 teaspoon margarine
1 Kokanee salmon, 1–1¾ pounds (½–¾ kg), filleted
1 teaspoon lemon juice
¼ teaspoon curry powder
Salt and pepper, to taste

Cooking

1. Preheat the gas grill on high, or start 4–5 dozen briquettes. Grease a piece of aluminum foil with the margarine and place the fillets on it. Brush the fish with lemon juice and season with curry powder, salt, and pepper.
2. Place the tinfoil with the fish on the grill. Pull the top down on the grill, vents open, and cook over high heat for 1–1½ minutes. With a spatula, turn the fillets over and cook on the other side for about 30 seconds more, or until the fish flakes to the touch of the fork.

SALMON BAKE

Yield: 4–6 servings

Take a rainy day, when you can't go out to the barbecue without a wet suit, and make this Salmon Bake. It's so fast, you'd better have the salad made, the table set, and everybody fork in hand.

Ingredients

1–2 pounds (½–1 kg) fresh salmon steaks or fillets

2 tablespoons butter

1 teaspoon fresh dill, or ¼ teaspoon dried

Cooking

1. Line a baking pan with foil and spray with a light coat of oil. Arrange the fillets on the foil. Melt the butter and combine with the dill. Brush generously on the steaks.

2. Adjust oven rack about 6 inches (15 cm) below the broiler and preheat the oven to 350°F (175°C). Bake the fish 8 minutes. If fillets have not yet begun to turn pink, cook another 5–7minutes. (Cold fillets right out of the refrigerator take longer than room temperature ones.)

3. When the flesh just starts to turn from raw to pink, put your oven on broil.

4. Broil about 3 minutes or until the edges are slightly brown. But leave the oven door ajar a few inches; this will allow you to peek in often to be sure your fillets don't get too brown. Serve with lemon wedges.

Chum salmon (Photo by Sil Strung)

Sockeye Salmon with Hollandaise Sauce

Yield: 6–8 servings

Sockeye run 5–7 pounds (2½–3 kg) on average; pink salmon 3–5 pounds (1½–2½ kg). Use either, or any other salmon of similar size. The recipe splits the difference: it's designed for a 5-pound (2½-kg) fish.

Ingredients

1 small onion, sliced thin
½ cup (125 ml) celery, sliced thin
1 teaspoon parsley
½ bay leaf
½ teaspoon leaf thyme
3 peppercorns, whole
Pinch of dried rosemary
Pinch of tarragon leaves
½ cup (125 ml) dry vermouth
3 slices lime
1 salmon, 5 pounds (2½ kg), whole

Cooking

1. Place all the ingredients except the fish in a medium-sized sauce pan. Simmer gently for 20 minutes. The vegetables will be limp.
2. Preheat oven to 425°F (220°C). Line a large roasting pan with heavy-duty aluminum foil. Place the fish in the foil, pull up the edges to make a boat. Pour the dry vermouth mixture over the fish. Seal tightly.
3. Bake in the oven, allowing 10 minutes per 1 inch (2½ cm) of thickness, measured at its thickest part. Do not disturb while baking.
4. To serve, remove the fish from the pan, put on a serving platter and serve with Hollandaise sauce.

Hollandaise Sauce

Ingredients

2 egg yolks
½ teaspoon salt
Dash of cayenne
½ cup (125 ml) butter
1 tablespoon lemon juice

Preparation

1. Place egg yolks in a medium-sized mixing bowl. Beat on high setting until the yolks become thick and turn lighter yellow. Add the salt and cayenne. Melt the butter almost to a boil in a separate saucepan.
2. Continue beating the egg mixture as you add—alternately—the butter and lemon juice. Add 2 tablespoons butter first, then 1 teaspoon lemon juice, and repeat until used up.
3. Serve over the salmon.

Note: If the sauce gets too cold while waiting for the salmon, reheat in a double boiler over low heat. Do not microwave or boil: the sauce will curdle.

Bass or Trout Ceviche

Yield: 4–6 servings

At our winter home near Altata, Mexico, when our Mexican friends go fishing they carry limes in their pockets that they use for everything from eye wash to antiseptic. When they catch a fish they can prepare their dinner without fire or pots. They clean the fish and put it in a small bowl, then squeeze the juice of the limes over it. As soon as the lime juice hits the flesh, the fish changes from pink to opaque right before your eyes, "cooking" the fish. Dinner—with no fire, pan, or fuss. For this recipe, bass are easier to fillet than trout, but trout work just fine.

Ingredients

1 pound (½ kg) fish, cut into ½ inch (1 cm) pieces or smaller
1 cup (250 ml) lime juice, freshly squeezed
1 teaspoon canned chilies, minced
½ teaspoon chili juice
2 tomatoes, chopped
½ red onion, minced
2 tablespoons chopped olives
2 tablespoons minced celery
½ teaspoon pepper
1 teaspoon salt

Preparation

1. Place the fish in a glass bowl. Add the lime juice, chilies, and chili juice. Mix well. Add the tomatoes, onion, olives, celery, and pepper, stirring gently to combine. Sprinkle the salt evenly over the top. Cover with plastic wrap and chill at least 1 hour.
2. Stir thoroughly but gently, and serve over crackers or tortilla chips.

Ceviche (Photo by Sil Strung)

EASY MICROWAVE WALLEYE

Yield: 2–4 servings

In the mid-1970s, my friends Jeanne and Eli Spannagel lived miles from a restaurant, and so they indulged themselves by buying the first microwave in Rosebud County. I had brought them some walleye as a present; Jeanne wanted to show off her brand-new kitchen appliance. A recipe was born. They still live miles from a restaurant, and they still fix Easy Microwave Walleye.

Ingredients

2 tablespoons cornstarch
3 tablespoons lemon juice
1 tablespoon dried parsley
$\frac{1}{4}$ teaspoon celery salt
Pinch of garlic salt
Pinch of pepper
$\frac{1}{2}$ cup (125 ml) butter, melted
2 pounds (1 kg) of walleye fillets

Preparation

1. In a medium-size bowl, add the cornstarch, lemon juice, and spices to the melted butter.
2. Dip the fillets in this batter and then place them in an oven-proof, microwave dish. Arrange the fillets so the thicker edges are facing out. Cover with plastic wrap.

Cooking

1. Microwave on high setting for 14–16 minutes in a 500-watt oven and 8 minutes in a 700-watt unit.
2. To serve, let the dish sit for 5 minutes, then serve with lemon wedges.

SANDWICHED PIKE

Yield: 6–8 servings

On a trip to northern Canada we caught a 27-pound (12-kg) pike. It fed the guide, his family of four, and the six of us. No matter the size of pike you have, this recipe makes a great one-dish meal with no cleanup.

Ingredients

2 tablespoons butter or margarine
2 large pike fillets, 14–16 inches (35–40 cm) long
$\frac{1}{2}$ teaspoon garlic salt
$\frac{1}{2}$ teaspoon pepper
1 pound ($\frac{1}{2}$ kg) package frozen hash browned potatoes, thawed
1 cup (250 ml) catsup
2 large onions, thinly sliced
1 can sauerkraut, 16 ounces (454 g), drained

Preparation

1. Preheat a propane barbecue to medium or start 4–5 dozen briquettes. Grease the center of a sheet of aluminum foil with butter and place one of the fillets on it. Sprinkle the fillet with half the garlic salt and pepper.
2. Spread half of the hash browned potatoes on the fillet; follow with a layer of half the catsup, then half the onions. Top this with the whole can of sauerkraut, which becomes the middle of the stack.
3. Now, reverse the order using the rest of the onions, catsup, and ending with the potatoes. Top with the other fillet and sprinkle with the remaining salt and pepper.
4. Seal the fish in the foil leaving about 1 inch ($2\frac{1}{2}$ cm) on top for the steam to escape.

Cooking

1. Place foil package on the barbecue and cook with the lid closed for 35–45 minutes, or until the fish flakes with a fork. When ready to serve, cut into individual portions.

STRIPED BASS CHOWDER

Yield: 10–15 servings

With potatoes, onions, a creamy base, and your own fresh-caught fish, you can have a real New England chowder with your own catch.

Ingredients

1 striped bass, or other saltwater white-fleshed fish, 10–12 pounds (4½–5½ kg), whole
3 pounds (1½ kg) potatoes, cut in 1-inch (2½-cm) cubes
¼ pound (100 g) bacon, diced
1 pound (½ kg) onions, chopped
3–4 cups (750–1000 ml) milk
1 tablespoon fresh or dried dill weed, or more to taste
3 tablespoons butter
3 tablespoons flour
Salt and pepper, to taste
1 lemon, freshly squeezed

Cooking

1. Clean and scale the fish. Remove the fillets and set them aside for another meal. Take the remaining heads, tails, and bones and place them in a large kettle. Cover with water and simmer for 45 minutes. Cool, then discard the bones but save any meaty chunks that fell of the bones, and return them to the pot. To this soup stock, add the potatoes and cook until they are tender.

2. In a separate saucepan, sauté the bacon, then the onions, and add to the potato and fish mixture, and continue to simmer on a back burner. Add the milk and enough of the dill to suit your taste; I like dill a lot, and use at least 1 tablespoon in soups.

3. Melt the butter in a separate saucepan, and stir in the flour to blend. When it's smooth, stir in some of the liquid from the chowder—enough to make it a thick sauce. Add this roux to the chowder pot. Stir and cook until the chowder thickens slightly.

4. To serve, add salt and pepper to taste and a dash of lemon juice.

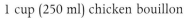

CRAWFISH PIE

Yield: 6–8 servings

The fun part of this recipe is to take a morning or afternoon off from the usual household chores and go out and collect these mini-lobsters. In the spring, they spawn in the shallows where you can gather them up by the bushel-full.

Ingredients

3 cups (750 ml) crawfish tails
3 cups (750 ml) cooked rice
½ cup (125 ml) chopped celery
½ cup (125 ml) chopped green bell peppers
1 bunch green onions, chopped
½ cup (125 ml) butter
¼ cup flour
2 cups (500 ml) milk

1 cup (250 ml) chicken bouillon
¼ pound (100 ml) mushrooms, sliced
½ teaspoon salt
⅛ teaspoon pepper
⅛ teaspoon cayenne
4 hard-boiled eggs, finely chopped
1 cup (250 ml) bread crumbs
¼ teaspoon paprika

Boiled crawfish for Crawfish Pie
(Photo by Sil Strung)

Preparation

1. Clean the crawfish by scalding in hot water for 5 minutes, drain, and cool. When cool, remove the tail from the body and peel off the skin.
2. Cook the rice and set aside.

Cooking

1. Over medium heat, sauté the celery, bell pepper, and green onions in the butter until wilted. Add the flour and stir until all the veggies are well coated. Add the milk, slowly, 1 cup (250 ml) at a time, raising the heat, briefly, to bring it to a simmer. The gravy will be thick: stir well, to avoid sticking. Add the bouillon. Preheat the oven to 350°F (175°C).
2. When the liquids are well mixed and back to a simmer, add the crawfish, cooked rice, and mushrooms. Pour this mixture into a greased baking dish and season with the salt, black pepper, and cayenne.
3. Evenly distribute the eggs and bread crumbs over the top, then sprinkle with the paprika over all. Bake uncovered at 350°F (175°C) for 30 minutes.
4. Serve with a green salad and French bread.

INDEX

ABOUT THE AUTHORS

Photo © by John Barsness

Photo © by Eileen Clarke

Eileen Clarke combines her three loves in this cook-book: hunting, writing, and experimenting with food. Her many articles on hunting, conservation, and natur-al history have appeared in numerous magazines, in-cluding *Field & Stream, Gray's Sporting Journal, Wyo-ming Wildlife, Shooting Sportsman,* and *Montana Out-doors.* She won first place prizes from the Outdoor Writer's Association of America in 1993 and 1995 for her articles. Her first novel, *The Queen of the Legal Ten-der Saloon,* will be published next year. In the mean-time, she's applying for moose, sheep, and antelope permits, tuning up her bow, stringing her new six-foot fly rod, and going bear hunting.

Sil Strung lives in a log cabin in Montana, where she hunts and fishes, and cooks what she brings home. She has taught in a one-room schoolhouse, worked as a fishing and hunting guide, and written and photo-graphed a cuisine column on wild game cookery for *Game Journal.* With Norman Strung, she is the co-author of the book *Camping in Comfort,* and has con-tributed to other books, including *To Catch a Trout, The Hunter's Almanac,* and *Hunter's Catalog.*